SPAIN & PORTUGAL

Iberian Portrait

The Plaza de España

SPAIN & PORTUGAL

Iberian Portrait

Daniel M. Madden

Thomas Nelson & Sons

All photographs are by Daniel M. Madden with the exception of the following: p. 204, Casa de Portugal, Portuguese Information and Tourist Office, 570 Fifth Avenue, New York, New York; p. 207, Spanish National Tourist Office, 589 Fifth Avenue, New York, New York. Permission is gratefully acknowledged.

The latest official decisions respecting the spelling of place names have been honored. The present official native language is used, except where usage has established a conventional form.

For Huan

All rights reserved under International and Pan-American Conventions. Published in Camden, N.J., by Thomas Nelson & Sons and simultaneously in Toronto, Canada, by Thomas Nelson & Sons (Canada) Limited.

Design by Harold Leach

Library of Congress Catalog Card Number: 69-15225

Printed in the United States of America

4

Foreword

One of the gentle ironies of history is that the countries which were responsible for the discovery of the New World are now themselves being discovered by the discovered. It is true they have long been on the map and in the news. But only in recent years have large numbers of Americans had the opportunity to set foot on the Iberian peninsula, meet the people, eat their food, sample their hospitality, and experience a different way of life. In the overwhelming majority of cases people of the New World have been happy to meet Spain and her neighbor, Portugal.

I am in that group. I like Spain. I like Spain very much. It is a friendship that has been growing for a long time—long enough for me to know the country, and long enough for me to learn that I would never become indifferent to her warm appeal.

I first became acquainted with Spain 20 years ago when my wife and I crossed the French-Spanish border at Port Bou and made the classic, memorable drive along the Costa Brava. In those days we had the road practically to ourselves. *Turismo* had not yet entered into the everyday Spanish vocabulary, and Spain was not on the itineraries of travel agencies.

This past summer, when my wife and I concluded another visit in Spain, the line of tourists crossing the border at Port Bou after their Spanish holiday was continuous. The border-crossers were of all nationalities, too. They were returning home with fine suntans and, more important, much to tell their relatives and friends.

Everyone might agree that Spain and Portugal are fine places to visit, but each visitor has a set of reasons that are almost as individualistic as fingerprints. Getting acquainted with a foreign land is a personal experience, and this is reflected in the way people tell about it. I have sought to make this book about Spain and Portugal comprehensive and objective, but it necessarily mirrors my own views based on many experiences during many visits over a 20-year period.

Some provinces of Spain have been treated briefly in the text, or even neglected entirely, while others may appear to be over-emphasized. My purpose was to produce a portrait of Spain and Portugal that was recognizable. The lack of space and the size of the task prevent the profile from being thor-

5

oughly fleshed out in all details, yet it is hoped that the outlines are sharp and vivid enough to effect a greater understanding of the Iberian peninsula, and of the tremendous potential for good represented in today's young generation of Iberians.

Restrictions on space prohibit a complete list of all the people of Spain and Portugal—men, women, and youths—who have helped me in developing this book, but there is room for each one of them in my memory.

I wish to thank in particular Professor José Garrut, sub-director of the City of Barcelona Museum; Esteban Bassols, of the City of Barcelona administration; Enrique Wúlff Martín, chief of the tourism office, Granada; Eduardo Molina Fajardo, director of the newspaper *Patria,* Granada; Rufo Gamazo Rico, editor in chief of *Arriba,* Madrid; Dr. F. Gómez Anton and Prof. José Luis G-Simancas, of the University of Navarre; Felipe de Ugarte, information delegate at San Sebastián; Prof. José Antonio Pero-Sans Elorz, of the Advanced School for Industrial Engineering, San Sebastián; Alvaro Cunqueiro, director of the newspaper *Faro del Vigo,* Vigo; Fernando de Castro Pires de Lima, director of the Museum of Ethnography and History, Oporto; Alexandro Armesto, counsellor of the Spanish Embassy, Rome; Suzanne Chantal, of Paris, who took the time from her busy writing schedule to give me her views and insights on Portugal about which she has written so well; and my wife, Huan, an unending source of knowledge, of aid, and of encouragement.

Daniel M. Madden

Paris, November, 1968

6

IBERIAN PENINSULA

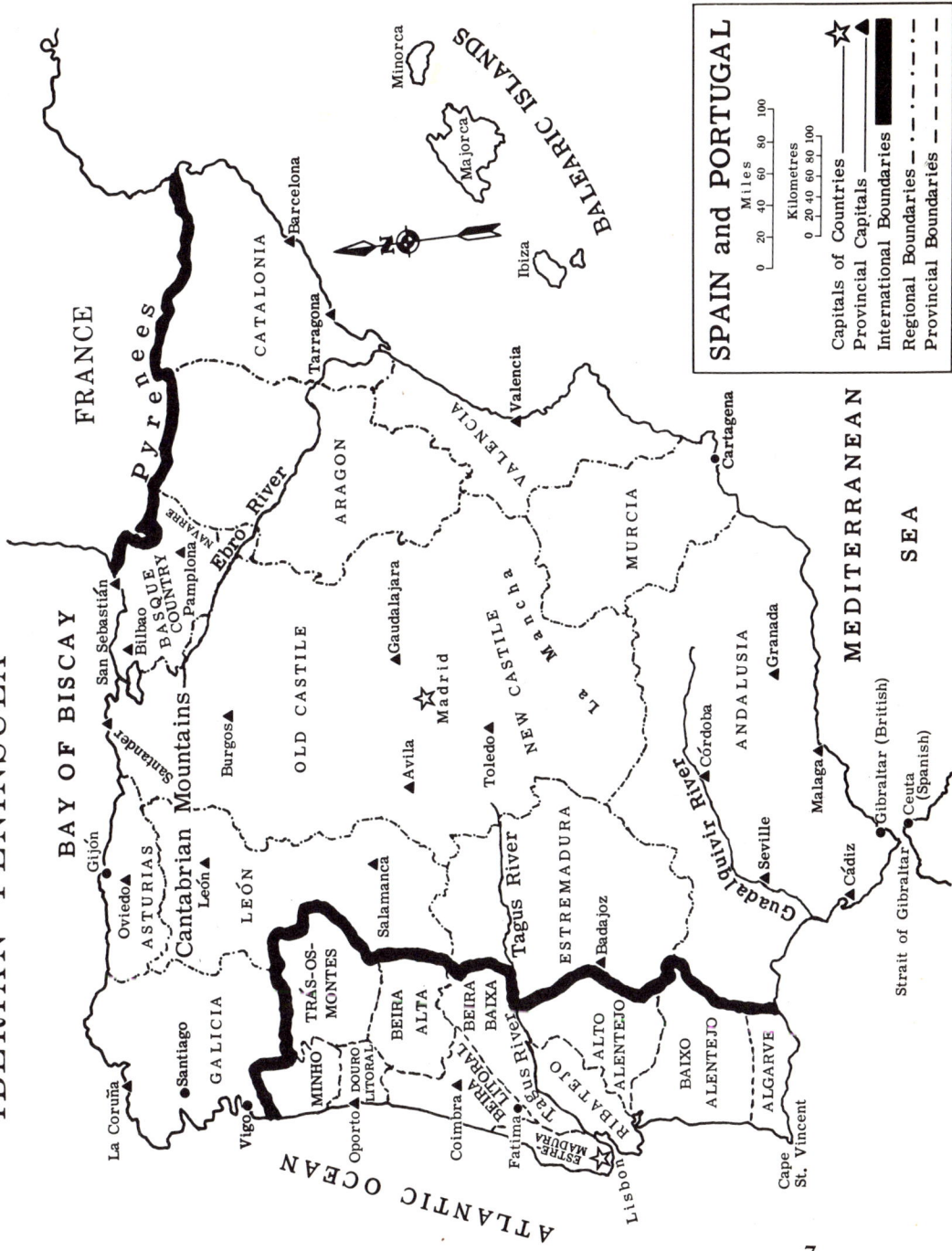

FRANCE

BAY OF BISCAY

ATLANTIC OCEAN

MEDITERRANEAN SEA

Pyrenees

Cantabrian Mountains

Ebro River

Tagus River

Guadalquivir River

Douro River

Minho River

BALEARIC ISLANDS

Minorca

Majorca

Ibiza

Spain regions
CATALONIA
ARAGON
NAVARRE
BASQUE COUNTRY
OLD CASTILE
NEW CASTILE
La Mancha
VALENCIA
MURCIA
ANDALUSIA
ESTREMADURA
LEÓN
ASTURIAS
GALICIA

Portugal regions
TRÁS-OS-MONTES
MINHO
DOURO LITORAL
BEIRA ALTA
BEIRA LITORAL
BEIRA BAIXA
ESTREMADURA
RIBATEJO
ALTO ALENTEJO
BAIXO ALENTEJO
ALGARVE

Cities
Barcelona
Tarragona
Valencia
Cartagena
Pamplona
Bilbao
San Sebastián
Santander
Gijón
Oviedo
Burgos
Gaudalajara
Madrid
Avila
Toledo
Córdoba
Granada
Seville
Malaga
Cádiz
Gibraltar (British)
Ceuta (Spanish)
La Coruña
Santiago
Vigo
Oporto
Coimbra
Fatima
Lisbon
Salamanca
León
Badajoz
Cape St. Vincent
Strait of Gibraltar

Legend
SPAIN and PORTUGAL

Miles
0   20   40   60   80   100

Kilometres
0   20 40 60 80 100

Capitals of Countries ☆
Provincial Capitals ▲
International Boundaries
Regional Boundaries —·—·—
Provincial Boundaries — — —

7

Contents

Statue in front of the cathedral at Oporto honors Vimara Peres for his defeat of the Moors

The New-Old Iberian Peninsula

People of Tarragona, looking for something to do after dinner besides sitting in a sidewalk café or going to a movie, had two possibilities one recent summer evening. The *Circo Milano*, a colorful assemblage of gypsy wagons and motor-drawn trailers with Rome license plates, had set up its tents in classic circus style on the empty ground alongside the sun-bleached Iberian-Roman walls of the third century B.C. That was one possibility. The other was the spectacle in the Plaza de Toros on the edge of the city. There, the "Holiday on Ice" company, using as a stage an ice rink spread across more than 1,000 square yards, was presenting *The Adventures of Marco Polo*, featuring "100 skaters, 300 fabulous costumes, and the most delicious music."

This was the first appearance of the world-known ice show in Tarragona, posters said. The circus from Italy did not mention how many times it, or some other magical agglomeration of wild animals, acrobats, and happy clowns, had been in the Spanish city on the Mediterranean before. No one would have any idea, for that matter, when the people of Tarragona saw their first circus. The first time might have been a couple of thousand years ago because the Romans liked circuses and Tarragona was once the capital of Hispania Citerior, that part of the Roman empire which included the mountainous north of present-day Portugal and the northern part of Spain, and which stretched from Galicia on the Atlantic to the Mediterranean.

Both the circus and the ice show drew big crowds during their short runs. The circus, presented in the afternoon, was popular with women

Monument of Queen Isabella and Christopher Columbus marks the center of Granada, where the discoverer received aid for his voyage to America

and children, but the hit of the season for Tarragona families was "Holiday on Ice." Its promoters obviously knew Spanish preferences. Their show was suited for the whole family—*todos los públicos*, as the throwaways said—and this is something important in Spain. The starting time for the two-and-one-half-hour performance was also synchronized with Spanish habits. The show *began* at 11 p.m. Staging this merry un-Spanish type of spectacle in the city's bull ring was an inspired way for bringing together something new and something old, and making everyone feel comfortable and satisfied.

Past and Present

Spaniards like tradition, but they also are eager to know what is new. They are as excited about a nuclear reactor going into operation in Guadalajara province as in the latest discovery of paintings on the wall of a prehistoric cave near Málaga. The city of Tarragona is a striking example of the combining of the traditional and the contemporary. The former Roman capital has become a leading international tourism center in modern-day Spain, and is also swiftly passing from a languid agricultural economy to a high-speed industralized

Iberian-Roman walls of the third century B.C. *at Tarragona, the capital of northern Spain and Portugal during the Roman occupation*

one. Some books speak of Tarragona as having a population of a million at the time of the Romans, but this could not be so because only 35,000 at most could crowd inside the city walls which were erected on foundations laid by the Iberians, the first known settlers of the area. It is more likely that the million referred to were the people under the jurisdiction of Tarragona, rather than the city's population. Even the size of today's population is hard to pin down. The official figure is 45,000 inhabitants—but that count was made two years ago, and that is a long time back for modern Tarragona. The real figure must be closer to 60,000.

And rising! Tourism and industrial planning are pushing Tarragona beyond its city limits of a few years ago, and new areas are being annexed. Tourists pay 10 pesetas to walk solemnly, almost on tiptoes, along the Archaeological Promenade of the Iberian-Roman walls, and earnestly study the Minerva Tower, the Cyclopean Gateway, and other features of the antique defense system of the town. Municipal authorities, meanwhile, map urbanization programs with officials from Madrid and stake out areas where public housing projects for 25,000 additional inhabitants can be built. Tourists stroll along the tree-filled Rambla of the Generalissimo, the main street that is named after General Franco, to the "Balcony of the Mediterranean" to watch the bobbing swimmers and the skittering motorboats in the blue water at Tarragona's front door. Municipal authorities, from the same vantage point, show businessmen the vast port area, the abundance of fresh water and electricity at the doorway of its fast-growing industrial zone, the easy, extensive rail and road communications to Barcelona, Madrid, or anywhere, and the fast loading-unloading facilities on the piers; they tell them about such things as the Liberian tanker *Atlantic Union* which on a recent afternoon arrived from Maracaibo with 32,000 tons of Venezuelan crude oil, discharged the cargo in a few hours, and began its return voyage.

The aqueduct stretching across a valley on the outskirts of Tarragona and the ruins of the Roman amphitheater encourage visitors to talk and think about life as it was here 20 centuries ago. Municipal officials

13

Remains of a Roman aqueduct at Mérida, former Lusitanian capital

say they are planning the space, landscape, and services needed for Tarragona of the year 2000. Tarragona remains international. During the summer Radio Tarragona broadcasts in French, English, Italian, and German to the tourists, telling them about places to visit, and where to eat and to shop.

Signs of the Romans can be seen today in the features of the people of Tarragona themselves, particularly the farmers, and in the trinity of usages which they left not only in Tarragona but everywhere on the Iberian peninsula—language, the cultivation of the vine, and the Christian religion. A statue of St. Paul, erected in 1963, inside the walls near the cathedral, honors the nineteenth centenary of the apostle's visit to Spain and his sojourn in Tarragona. Each civilization has left its mark on the peninsula, although some more distinctly than others.

There are those who say you can often tell the distant origins of the inhabitants of small, out-of-the-way villages by the color of their houses because the habits of people change slowly even when time is measured in centuries. The Greeks painted their houses blue; the Romans, a terracotta red; the Moors, white. Some of the earliest inhabitants of

14

the Iberian peninsula did not live in conventional dwellings, but they left their imprints in interesting ways, nonetheless. The Iberian peninsula has been lived in for a long time!

The Mainland and Beyond

Spain covers an area of 190,190 square miles which can be an abstract, almost meaningless figure unless you consider that its area is one-thousandth of the earth's entire surface, something like one twentieth of the European continent, and five sixths of the Iberian peninsula. That leaves a little less than 38,000 square miles for its neighbor, Portugal. Spain's size makes it the third largest country in Europe. Its mountains give it another interesting distinction. After Switzerland, whose Alps put the Swiss in top position, Spain has a higher average altitude (2,000 feet) than any other continental nation.

The Iberian peninsula is one of three major points of land that jut into the Mediterranean from the European continent, and it is easily larger than the Italian and Greek peninsulas. As in the classic definition, the Iberian peninsula is almost entirely surrounded by water—the Mediterranean on the east, southeast, and south; the Atlantic on the southwest, west, and north—and is connected with the mainland of Europe by a solid, 415-mile isthmus, the Pyrenees.

Outside the Iberian peninsula the territory of Portugal includes: in the Atlantic, the Madeira and Azores Islands, which are near enough to be considered as an adjacent part of the nation; in West Africa, the Cape Verde Islands, Guinea, Angola, Gabinda, and certain smaller possessions; in East Africa, Mozambique; in Oceania, the island of Timor and its dependencies; and on the Asian mainland, Macao. Portugal also considers that it continues to possess Goa, on the southwest coast of India, which was occupied by Indian forces in 1961.

The Spanish territory outside the mainland is nowhere near as extensive, or as much of a political headache, as Portugal's. It consists of three island provinces (the Balearics in the Mediterranean, and Las Palmas and Tenerife in the Canary group in the Atlantic) and two African provinces (Ifni and Spanish Sahara) plus the North African cities of Ceuta and Melilla. Among the islands in the Balearic group are Majorca, Minorca, and Ibiza, which are extremely popular with tourists. The Canaries, off the northwest coast of Africa, are the "blessed islands of the Hesperides," where golden apples grew in a wondrous garden and were guarded by lovely nymphs.

Ancient Iberians and Rock Art

Great rivers flow across the Iberian mainland, most of them emptying into the Atlantic on the western coast. But the celebrated river with which the ancient inhabitants of the peninsula are associated rises in the north and flows eastward into the Mediterranean, between Tarragona and Valencia. This is the Ebro, or the Iberus, as it used to be known, and the name Iberian was applied to the early-day people who inhabited the eastern part of the peninsula.

The Iberians were a mysterious people, who lived atop mountains to protect themselves, and not much is known about them. Where they came from, and even when, are still big question marks. Perhaps they originated in central Europe, or somewhere in southern Europe. A new theory is that they migrated through North Africa, crossed into the peninsula at Gibraltar, and then headed north along the eastern side of present-day Spain.

In the sixth century B.C. the Celts came from the north and occupied the northwestern part of Spain and the northern part of Portugal. When the Celts moved eastward and the Iberians traveled westward they formed a new people called the Celt-Iberians who lived in the center of the peninsula. Meantime, while the Iberians (and later, the Celts) settled somewhat inland from the sea, seagoing Phoenicians and Greeks were establishing coastal trading centers. In the eleventh century B.C. the Phoenicians founded the seaport of Cádiz which, at the time, was deep in the domain of another ancient people, the Tartesos, who are known to us only through Greek writers.

Spain's history is literally in its art, and it is a story that has only recently begun to unfold. We know something about the Iberians by the paintings they did on the walls of their caves. They are of human figures—hunters, dancers—general scenes, and the like. These caves were not very deep and the paintings are relatively near the entrance.

16

A dam on the Ebro River in the province of Tarragona, west of Mora la Nueva

In the Ebro Valley, in the village of Cogul which is near Lérida, one of the Iberian cave paintings features a woman doing a fertility dance. These paintings, it is believed, were done around the year 10,000 B.C. Similar paintings have been found in the moutains near Tarragona and down along the coast—near Castellón, Valencia, and Murcia, for instance. New discoveries are being made all the time.

The first example of this rock art was discovered at the end of the nineteenth century along the north coast at Altamira in the Castilian province of Santander. Because of the superb paintings, Altamira is described as "The Sistine Chapel of Prehistoric Art." There was much controversy about the Altamira discovery at first, with some people asserting that the paintings were false. But a French expert on prehistoric art, Abbé Breuil, inspected the Spanish cave and certified that its paintings were genuine.

These first paintings were of a bison, and the animal design of the painting is now reproduced on the package of a popular Spanish

17

cigarette. After this discovery at Altamira, other paintings were found in Spanish grottoes which are believed to be as much as 25,000 or 30,000 years old. These very ancient masterpieces are always of animals—bison, deer, and bulls, in general. Not long ago, near Santander, paintings of an elephant were found in a cave. In these prehistoric times people lived deep in dry caves because glaciers coated the ground. Some people are amazed that man could have painted so well and so surely in this Paleolithic period, but the rock-art discoveries, and their authentication by the experts, demonstrate that he could indeed. Later, during the Neolithic period, man graduated from the animal to the human figures we see in the Iberian caves of the Ebro Valley.

The Carthaginians

The Celt-Iberians had the peninsula pretty much to themselves until the arrival of the Carthaginians who, after occupying the Phoenician

Clay pit where bricks are made near Mérida

colonies on the southern shore in the sixth century B.C., conquered the entire south and southeastern parts of Spain over a 20-year period in the third century B.C. Their main arrival point was at Cartagena, which today is the headquarters of the Spanish naval forces in the Mediterranean.

Hardly had the Carthaginians completed their occupation in the year 218 B.C. when the Romans appeared on the scene, and entered Spain to battle their rivals. Rome and Carthage were struggling for control of the Mediterranean and were to fight three Punic wars over it. The Second Punic War was fought on the peninsula, when the Romans arrived; and after it the Romans and Carthaginians worked out a treaty, fixing the Ebro as the dividing line between their domains. The Carthaginians were to remain south of the Ebro, according to the agreement. But Hannibal defied the Romans, and coming up from the south passed behind the mountains of Barcelona, which was a small village at the time, crossed the Pyrenees, and then moved through the Alps. The Romans shrewdly sought a change of venue for the war, switching it to Africa, and there in 146 B.C. the Third Punic War put an end to the fortunes of the Carthaginians and left the Romans free to colonize the entire Iberian peninsula.

Romans, Visigoths, and Moors

The Romans met very stiff resistance from the Celt-Iberians, a people preferring death to subjugation, and it took bribery as well as brawn to conquer the peninsula. The Lusitanians—the descendants of Celtic tribes that had settled in the central part of Portugal and as far south as the Algarve—were overrun by the Romans in 185 B.C. but it was not until 38 B.C., almost two centuries after they had first cast their eye on the peninsula as a good place to colonize, that the Romans were in complete control. Tarragona then became the capital for the northern part of the peninsula. Lusitania and the southern part of Spain, Baetica (now Andalusia), were grouped together in Hispania Ulterior. Emerita, the present Spanish city of Mérida (which is near Badajoz and the Spanish-Portuguese border) was made the capital of Lusitania.

In the early part of the fifth century Germanic barbarian tribes began filtering through the Pyrenees. The Romans by this time were already in decline, and they welcomed the newcomers as allies, assigning them territories on the peninsula.

The four principal barbarian tribes were the Swabians, who settled in the northern part of Portugal and in Galicia (the northwest part of present-day Spain); the Vandals, who occupied Andalusia; the Alanos who moved into Castile; and the Visigoths, or West Goths as they also were known. The Visigoths arrived in A.D. 414, five years after the first wave of the barbarians and in a half century made Spain their kingdom, choosing Toledo as their capital. The Visigoths were more civilized than the other tribes and, although Christians, had adopted the heresy of Arianism while they were in the eastern half of the Roman empire. (Arianism took its name from a priest of Alexandria, Arius, who in the fourth century taught that the Second Person of the Trinity, God the Son, is not really God in the sense in which the Father is God). The Arianism of the Visigoths clashed with the orthodox Catholicism left with the inhabitants of the peninsula by the Romans, and it was a divisive factor for a time. One early Visigothic king, Leovigildo, ordered the killing of a son who had become a Catholic. Leovigildo was subsequently succeeded as king by another son, Recaredo who, with his queen, Baddo, renounced Arianism during the Third Council of Toledo in 589. By their act Catholicism became the official religion, and from then on would be part of Spanish—as well as Portuguese—life and history.

After two and a half centuries the Visigothic kingdom abruptly ended with the sudden invasion of the Arabic-speaking, Moslem people called the Moors, who were a mixture of Arabs from the Middle East and Berbers of North Africa. The Moors invaded Spain in 711 by crossing the less than ten miles of sea in the Strait of Gibraltar that separates Africa from Europe, and swarmed across the peninsula. Within a scant half-dozen years they took everyone and everything into their possession, except for a few pockets of resistance in the northern mountains. The Reconquest was started immediately in 718 in Asturias, but it went on for centuries. Portugal was finally seized from the Moors almost five centuries to the day after the Reconquest began, while it took almost eight centuries for all of Spain to be won back. Crusaders from France, England, and other countries joined in the endeavor because, after all, this was a confrontation of the Cross and the Crescent. But it was not a holy war altogether, and among the outside helpers were adventurers and those with property-aggrandizement and other selfish interests in mind.

Iberian Conquests and Losses

As the Reconquest gained momentum, the Christian conquerors established independent kingdoms in Spain, and one of the early-day powerful rulers was the king of León and Castile whose rule reached westward across present-day Portugal. ("We had kings before Madrid had laws," the people of León say.) A French Crusader, a Burgundian nobleman who had been entrusted with the area of northern Portugal, declared his independence early in the twelfth century from the king of León, and his son, Afonso Henriques, later formally proclaimed himself king of the new independent County of Portucale. Afonso strengthened his hold on the title by defeating the Moors in an important battle at Ourique in 1139, and links with León and Castile were broken once and for all. This is generally considered as the time of the founding of the kingdom of Portugal although it was not until forty years later, in 1179, that the Pope formally recognized Afonso as king.

Relations between Spain and Portugal have been on a love-hate basis ever since, and they have engaged in formal, full-dress battles at various times. Recently Portugal unveiled at Batalha a statue to its soldier-hero, Nuño Alvares Pereira, who defeated the Spaniards in 1385.

Explorers from Spain and Portugal roamed the world, starting early in the fifteenth century, and brought their countries wealth and power. An expedition led first by the Portuguese Magellan and continued, after Magellan's death, by the Spanish Basque Elcano brought back proof by circumnavigating the globe in the early part of the sixteenth century that the earth was round. In 1500 Pedro Alvares Cabral discovered Brazil for Portugal, and in the same year another Portuguese explorer,

Gaspar Corte Real arrived at Greenland. Hernan Cortes, who was born in the Spanish province of Cáceres (called "the Land of the Conquistadores") conquered Mexico in 1522 and christened it New Spain. In the Western Hemisphere cities from St. Augustine to Lima to Buenos Aires were founded by Spaniards. The culture of western Europe spread to the Americas with Spanish and Portuguese explorers, and the Spanish empire reached into Italy, Germany, and the Low Countries. The Philippines were incorporated into the Spanish empire in 1565, and six years later Spanish men-of-war joined naval forces of the Pope in defeating the Turks at the pivotal battle of Lepanto. Cervantes was among the Spanish fighting men, and among the wounded.

But the inevitable decline came. Early in the eighteenth century Spain lost her European possessions of Flanders, Milan, Sicily, and Sardinia, and in the middle of the century a devastating earthquake shattered Lisbon. The effects of the French Revolution reached into Spain and Portugal. Napoleon sent troops into Portugal, hoping to bring the country under France's sphere of influence and break the long-standing Anglo-Portuguese alliance. In the Americas, Spain was losing her colonies and Brazil declared its independence from Portugal. Liberal thoughts from France fanned the winds of change and in the latter part of the nineteenth century Isabella II was dethroned and the First Republic was proclaimed in Spain. In one year four people succeeded one another as president. After existing little more than a year the First Republic was ended with the restoration of the monarchy in 1874 and the proclamation of Alfonso XII as king. These were just some of the bad blows that kept hitting the two Iberian neighbors.

Political Disquiet

Anti-clericalism in Portugal, which started in the middle of the eighteenth century, gained momentum, and so did a revolutionary spirit and a general malaise. In 1908, King Carlos and his oldest son were assassinated as they were driving near the waterfront in Lisbon, and two years later his son, Manuel II, abdicated in order to avoid a civil war. A republic was proclaimed and between 1910 and 1926 there

A massive cross rises above an underground basilica, partially shown at right, in the Valley of the Fallen, a memorial to the dead of the Spanish Civil War

were 40 different governments and about half that many revolutions. Internal struggles impoverished the nation, and enriched the languages of the world with a new word, "portugalized," meaning something that had completely gone to pot.

Fed up with the way things were going, a group of military men took over the government in a coup d'état on May 28, 1926, and invited a middle-aged economics professor at Coimbra University, Dr. Antonio de Oliveira Salazar, to become minister of finance and rescue the nation from complete bankruptcy. Salazar wanted a free hand but

23

when this was not given him he resigned in a few days and went back to the classroom. But in 1928 he returned to the Portuguese cabinet as minister of finance, when he was assured broader powers, and four years later he became prime minister—and held the position until late in September, 1968.

National despondency, accumulating for several centuries, reached its nadir in Spain just before the end of the nineteenth century and great writers who came to be known as "The Generation of '98" joined in bemoaning the loss of Puerto Rico, Cuba, and the Philippines. Maria Cristina was queen of Spain at this time and her son, Alfonso XIII, was declared king in 1902 on reaching the age of 16. He was ruler only in name, however, and behind the scenes the generals and politicians were doing the manipulating. There are many dark stories of these times about rival power blocs hiring killers to do away with the opposition. In 1923 General Miguel Primo de Rivera mounted a coup d'état, and his dictatorship lasted until the depression. Alfonso XIII was ruling—or, at least, was king—during this hectic period.

But he saw the handwriting on the wall. Republican supporters won the municipal elections of April, 1931, in the big cities, although the monarchists piled up a good vote in the countryside. The king abdicated and the Second Republic was established. Separatist movements gained strength in Catalonia and the Basque country. Asturias was shaken by a bloody revolution in 1934 and the tremors spread across Spain; religious persecution broke out, and there was general chaos as one side tried to outdo the other in ferociousness. The chaotic situation was heightened by a militant force of anarchists who were against everyone and everything. A diplomat says that Spain at the time had a million anarchists.

In July of 1936 some army elements led by General Franco revolted, and the Civil War was started. It ended three years later after Spain had been wrecked, the spirit of its people broken, and perhaps as many as one million lives lost.

But Spaniards do not long remain despondent or despairing. Old values encourage and strengthen them, and they are not afraid to face the world or tomorrow. The horrors of the Civil War fade as economic progress continues.

The Iberian peninsula is almost one immense island, but its inhabitants have never had an insular outlook. They have been influenced by several waves of world civilizations and have in turn affected the lives of peoples elsewhere by opening up new routes of trade and exploration and by discovering new worlds to colonize. The colonial era brought fame and great wealth to the peninsula, but today's Iberians realize that their future depends on development within their own borders.

Today's Iberians

Present-day Spaniards, although as traditional in their values as their ancestors, have a contemporary outlook. It is difficult anywhere to pinpoint a *typical* family, but it is possible in Spain to identify families which typify this old-new, traditional-contemporary Spanish quality of adaptability. The family of Vicente Giner Beira is one of these. (*Giner* is his father's family name; *Beira*, his mother's).

A Spanish Lawyer

Señor Giner practices law in Valencia, the luxuriant, lovely Mediterranean city south of Tarragona, which is known for its belfries (Victor Hugo counted 300 of them), for its gardens, for its rice fields, and for the beauty of its women. Valencia is also famous for its *Tribunal de las Aguas* ("Irrigation Water Court") which is probably the oldest judicial assembly in the world. It might go back to the time of the Romans, who built the first canals, but its age at least can be traced to the year 960, which was in the middle of the Moorish occupation. Members of the Court are elected representatives of the farmers who use the irrigation water. The *Tribunal de las Aguas* handles all questions involving the misuse of the irrigation water by the farmers of the Valencia *huerta*, and its decisions are binding—and cannot be appealed.

Each Thursday at noon the seven judges—one for each of the main canals—meet in the doorway of the Valencia Cathedral, wearing the short black smocks which are the traditional work clothes of farmers

A milkman follows his donkey toward a gate of the city wall in Avila on a sunny but chilly morning

27

of the area. In the days of the Moors the Court met in the Grand Mosque which the Christians replaced with the present cathedral after James I seized Valencia in the thirteenth century. The Moors remaining in Valencia as farm workers after the city had returned to Christian hands did not wish to enter the temple of the Christians—and the Christians probably would not have let them, anyway—so the cathedral doorway was chosen as a compromise site for the courtroom. Señor Giner is the assessor, or counsellor for the Water Court. His father, before him, served as assessor for a half century. So much for tradition.

Distinguished is the word that best describes Señor Giner. His hair is graying, he has a small mustache, he dresses well, and he laughs easily. Señor Giner belongs to a luncheon group of business and professional men who meet once a month, in a different place each time, and eat something typical of the region. When the group was formed four years ago, the specialty on their menu that day was baby eels and that settled the problem of a name. The group calls itself El Mornell, the name of the hourglass-shaped net that is used for catching eels. The *mornell* is also the group's symbol, and on meeting-days members wear a gold lapel button which is a miniature of the eel net. The club button gets the meetings off to a merry start each month because members, as they arrive, are carefully scrutinized by one another.

Painted tiles spruce up a railroad station at Valencia

*Members of the ancient Tribunal de las Aguas begin a session of the farmers'
Irrigation Water Court at the doorway of the cathedral in Valencia*

Those who have forgotten to wear their *mornell* button must pay a
fine of 100 pesetas and these friendly fines, added to by voluntary
contributions from the several dozen members, are used for charity
work. The luncheon meeting is a leisurely one, starting at 2 p.m. and
lasting until 4:30 or 5 p.m. The group tries to pick not only places
where the food is good, but also which have some historic or artistic
background. The only serious business discussed at the monthly meetings of El Mornell is the site for the next get-together.

A Spanish Family

The Giner family lives in a second-floor apartment on a side street
within walking distance of the Valencia University. The entrance to
the apartment is shaped like a large L with a sitting-reception room
near the doorway and a dining-room adjoining it. It stretches out to
the rear of the building where, on a small, flowered balcony overlooking the garden, Señor Giner and his wife like to have breakfast on a

Part of the Vicente Giner family: (left to right) Vicente, Marta, Amparo, Dolores, Sonsoles, and Remedios

nice day. At the back of the apartment there is also a large family room, with a television set on rollers, a record player, and several comfortable chairs. Between the family room and the dining room is a series of bedrooms, and those used by the Giner daughters have dolls on the beds, We-Try-Harder buttons on the walls, the latest "pop" records on tables, and miscellaneous knick-knacks gathered by the older girls on trips to Dublin and Paris.

It is a big family—seven daughters, ranging in age from 13 to 26, and a 12-year-old son, named Vicente after his father. The daughters are classic Spanish beauties, full of spirit, and able to talk seriously or laugh merrily. Señor Giner says it was very nice when all the girls were

30

young and they used to sit in a circle and braid one another's hair. The oldest daughter, Maria-José, lives in Cádiz and is married to a naval engineer who has helped build 70,000- to 100,000-ton tankers; he is at work on a 150,000-tonner, and is studying plans for a 300,000-ton one. Dolores, 23, is a lawyer and works in her father's office. Isabel-Clara, 21, is studying exact sciences and is interested in entering the research field of mathematics and computers. She is named after the daughter of Philip II. ("He was the greatest king in all the world," Señor Giner says. "He loved his father very much and I loved my father very much, too.") Marta, 19, is enrolled at the Valencia University. She is a crackerjack horsewoman, and won the Valencia women's championship two years ago. The younger girls are Amparo, 13, a swimmer and a "pop" music fan; Remedios—or Reme—15, who began playing basketball when she was 12, and traveled to Belgium recently to compete in the finals for junior girls' basketball teams of the Federación Internacional Esportiva Colegios Católicos; and Sonsoles, 17, who has won a swimming medal and whose name comes from an ancient title for the Virgin, meaning that her eyes are "like the sun."

Amparo has not thought too much as yet as to what she is going to do when she grows up, and Remedios has not decided. It is hard to decide at 15, Señor Giner says. Sonsoles, two years older than Reme, is studying to be a social-service worker.

"There are many cases needing assistance and help," Sonsoles says, referring to a practical study her class is making in a Valencia district. "It is important to know these needs, but it is important, too, that the people should know where they can get help. Many people are ignorant of the resources which are available, and one of the things I want to do is to inform people where and how they can be helped. I might work in a hospital, or a school for subnormal children, or in a kindergarten for the children of factory workers. The kindergarten would be a good opportunity because it brings you into contact with the parents and then you could help mothers in choosing the right food, and diet, for their family; and with the hygiene for the home, and with the bringing up of the children—important things like that."

The Badajoz Plan

Social problems are important and the government is aware of the need for change. In 1945 Francisco Franco Bahamonde, *caudillo* ("leader") of Spain, head of state, and commander-in-chief of the armed forces of the nation, traveled to Badajoz, a brown hilly province where the most spectacular sight used to be the way the Guadiana River, strengthened by rills and rock-strewn streams, fought its way through narrow canyons to the Spanish-Portuguese border. Bajadoz, situated in a remote region of Spain fittingly known as Estremadura, is the nation's largest province. In the three decades Franco has ruled Spain he has made countless ceremonial visits to places near and far within the country, but the Badajoz journey was not in that category, as he explained at the time. He had come to Bajadoz, Franco bluntly said, because it presented the deepest social problem of all the provinces of Spain.

Since then, social conditions have dramatically improved. In much the same way that America's southwestern desertland was homesteaded

An umbrella provides shade for a traffic officer on duty at the stone gateway to the city of Badajoz in western Spain

One of the dams of the Guadiana River which store and supply water to irrigate agricultural lands under the Badajoz Plan. This dam is near Mérida

and irrigated, the province of Badajoz has blossomed into a livable, productive area now known in Spain for the high quality of its fruits and vegetables, the richness of its soil, and the determination of the settlers who have made the desert bloom. A galaxy of great dams, joined to a network of hundreds of miles of channels and canals, draw upon the waters of the Guadiana which once were ignored, and have opened up two vast agricultural areas: the Vegas Altas of 195,000 acres and, near the city of Badajoz and the border, the Vegas Bajas of 130,000 acres. Homesteaders have been given on easy terms ten or twelve acres of irrigated land, a modern house, farm equipment, and livestock; for each farm worker there is a house, with a half acre of land suitable for a vegetable garden.

A score of new villages have been created, others are under construction, and still others are planned. Each new *pueblo* includes a church, schools, clinic, clubrooms for women and for young people, offices for labor syndicates, a movie-house, and cooperative stores. The hills, once empty and bleak, have sprouted with young trees, like a super-

Homesteaders receive a house and farm buildings such as these, as well as land, equipment, and livestock under the Badajoz Plan

market nursery, as the result of a massive forestation program. New roads and rail lines have been built and old ones are being improved. Recently established industrial plants use and process in a modern, imaginative way the four basic products from the land: fruits, vegetables, textile fibers, and livestock. Irrigation has increased the value of the land's yield nearly ten times. This successful rechanneling of human and natural resources is known as the Badajoz Plan, the first in a series of postwar projects to put Spain on its feet economically and socially after it had been shaken to the core by the terrible Civil War.

As in Portugal, after the period of brother-against-brother fighting, authoritarianism brought political stability, and this was an immediate aim. But the long-range goal was for an across-the-board comprehensive stability, ranging from economic to social, which would repair the human and physical damage of war and give the new generation of Spaniards reason for hope and pride.

Spain's Image Abroad and at Home

The Badajoz Plan was not approved until 1952, seven years after Franco's visit to the lonely province. The interval was a busy and difficult one for Spain because in addition to improving conditions at home the government had to do something about its image abroad where many people associated it with political repression. Franco began to rebuild slowly, starting first with mending the political fabric. In the middle of July, 1945, the *Fuero de los Españoles,* defining the basic

34

human rights and responsibilities of the Spanish people, was approved. Another law, during that same year, granted a general amnesty to those persons who had held political positions during the Civil War. Abroad, in 1946, the newly established United Nations organization voted sanctions against Spain—in effect, boycotting and isolating her—and the United States and other nations withdrew their ambassadors. The biggest blow to Spain's postwar economic recovery was being kept out of the group of western European nations (which included Portugal) who were to receive billions of dollars from the United States under the Marshall Plan. This hurt Spain and her people, not only economically but psychologically. In 1950 the UN sanctions were called off, and two years later Spain was permitted to enter—not the UN itself—but, at least, a major arm of the international organization, UNESCO. Admission to the United Nations itself was held off till 1955.

Meanwhile, Spain worked out two important international agreements—both in the year 1953. A military accord with the United States

A Spanish trainman at Badajoz, where transportation facilities are being improved to keep up with the agricultural and industrial progress of the area

provided for the establishment of various installations and facilities, including the naval base at Rota, on the southwestern Atlantic flank of Spain not far from where Columbus set sail, which is said to be one of the world's biggest. The other agreement linked Spain once again with the Holy See in a new Concordat that replaced the 1851 one which the short-lived Second Republic had cancelled.

The Badajoz Plan was eventually followed in other under-developed areas by the systematic establishment of industrial and agricultural *polos,* which would polarize investment, development, and expansion activity, and serve as powerful, positive magnets for economic growth. The *polos,* bulwarked by government financial aid, tax relief, and other helpful props, were spaced throughout the country, being industrial or agricultural in a zone—or both—depending on the situation. For the agricultural group Badajoz remained the "granddaddy," while the steel-expansion program in Asturias became the leading industrial *polo.*

Labor Universities

The Universidad Laboral has been one of the most imaginative ways of developing the different areas of the nation by educating the sons and daughters of workers in trades and professions that can earn them

Underdeveloped areas such as Elda-Petrel, near Alicante in southeastern Spain, where houses are built into the hills, may be aided by the establishment of a government-subsidized polo *to raise the economy and standard of living*

a high standard of living and prepare them for going as far as they like, and are able, in technical careers. The term *universidad laboral* is a slight misnomer, since it is not a university in the classic sense and since it comes under the primary purview of the Ministry of Labor, rather than the Ministry of Education. But the labor university is definitely an institution of higher education for young people who, otherwise, might quit school at the age of fourteen and go into the working world with only a minimum of general education and no vocational training. There are ten of these labor universities in various parts of Spain, and others are planned.

Students at the labor universities continue their general education and at the same time are trained in a specialty which can vary from university to university. At Alcalá (Madrid) the specialty is electronics; in Seville, one of the main courses is electricity; at Zaragoza, a Universidad Laboral for girls, the students are taught to be assistants in chemical and industrial laboratories. Most of the construction costs of the labor universities have been financed by the *mutualidades,* the insurance funds of trade unions. A basic entrance requirement is that a student must be the son or daughter of a workingman who pays into a trade-union insurance fund, or is the child of someone who is retired because of physical disability, or who has been left an orphan by the death of a worker. The student must also meet scholastic requirements and pass an entrance examination. Students at these universities range in age from 14 or 15 to 21, or even a bit older in the case of those who have stayed on for advanced studies.

Courses are generally for three years at which time a student gets an *oficialiá*, certifying that he is a trained worker in a specified field and is capable of being a foreman. An electronics specialist, for instance, is allowed to call himself *oficial electronico* on completing his course and the title not only assures him a job but one at better than average pay —probably more than his father earns. If the youngster wishes to—and has the ability—he can study for a *maestria* rating, or for a degree as an industrial engineer. One of the most fascinating aspects of the Universidad Laboral program is that everything is free. That means *everything*—not just the tuition—from clothing to food!

Aerial view of the central courtyard of the immense labor university at Gijón, with its 393-foot Tower of Culture in the foreground

The average enrollment is around 1,000 but La Coruña has somewhat less than 350 students while more than 2,200 young boys are at the labor university in Madrid. Even bigger things are in store. The university to be built in Valencia before 1970 is to have an initial enrollment of 2,500 students and within two years that is expected to double. The newer universities are entirely in the hands of civilians, but four of the early ones are administered by religious orders. The Salesians (Society of Don Bosco) are at Zamora and Seville; the Dominicans at Córdoba; and the Jesuits at Gijón, which specializes in industrial mechanics and which was the first of the labor universities. There are 35 Jesuits at Gijón, including ten scholastics, in various administrative positions, and among them they have an interesting collection of secular degrees. The rector is a lawyer; the vice-rector has both law and industrial engineering degrees; the prefect of discipline is a graduate psychologist; one of the Jesuits is a chemical engineer; another is a physical scientist; and so on. The Jesuits do not teach any of the courses, but they do give some lectures—although they are not paid for this.

Gijón has been called the Escorial of the labor universities, and the title was not given without some thought. (The Royal Monastery of San Lorenzo de El Escorial, an enormous rectangular building measuring 175 by 225 yards, is a combination palace-church-royal burial place erected by Philip II in the sixteenth century to commemorate a victory over the French at St. Quentin.) Gijón is also an architectural masterpiece, and a very large one. In its general beauty, design, and workmanship it can hold its own with any full-fledged university in the world. Wooden doors to the rooms, after being slammed by husky teen-age boys innumerable times a day since school started in 1955, are as good as new. The granite and special stones with which it has been built look as if they could resist time.

Some statistics give an idea of why it is called the Escorial of labor universities, but cold facts do not do the title-givers justice. The roofing material consists of 387,513 square feet of blue slate that covers an area larger than the roof of the Escorial. Blue was chosen because such a vast area in the usual red would be irritating to the observer in the otherwise tranquil green countryside of Asturias. The church cupola weighs 2,300 tons. The central courtyard, which is paved with granite, covers the same area as St. Mark's Square in Venice—492 feet in length and 164 feet in width. The closest attention was given to design.

The 393-foot Tower ("Tower of Culture") was inspired by the Lighthouse of Alexandria, although it simultaneously is reminiscent of Seville's La Giralda. The height and width of the 2,000-seat theater are the same as those of the Parthenon. The workshops, which are the classrooms for the practical training of the students, occupy an area of 172,228 square feet and were inspired by the Baths of Caracalla. The entrance way to the university is through a Corinthian Atrium that was described 20 centuries ago by a Roman architectural historian named Vitruvius but which, except for a small scale version in Copenhagen, had never been built till this one at Gijón. The terrace and gardens bring to mind the Generalife of Granada. The main door of the church suggests the bronze doors on the Baptistery in Florence. Blue granite columns almost 36 feet high—the same height as those of the Parthenon—support the gallery of the Corinthian Atrium, and throughout the university there are 100 columns altogether.

In other words, the Universidad Laboral at Gijón is quite a place. Nearly as impressive as the architecture, for some people, is that almost every student has his own big room. The Jesuits, when first invited to administer the Gijón university were ready to say "no, thank you," because the quarters intended for them were relatively sumptuous and they feared this might go against their vow of poverty. When the Jesuits saw that the students would also have large, airy, nicely furnished private rooms, they decided to accept.

The grandeur and eloquent style of the Gijón labor university illustrates a fundamental characteristic of Spaniards. A village might be without a school, or a hospital, or a hotel a lot longer than it should, but when the Spaniards decide to build one it will be a superb prototype. The Escorial is an old example, and a newer one is the Valley of the Fallen, fifty kilometers from Madrid, which is a unique monument built by Franco to honor the dead of the Civil War and includes a giant cross and an underground basilica.

Rural Schools and Tele-Clubs

Young people in the agricultural villages—even those in the remotest, tiniest *aldeas*—have not been overlooked. For students who live in *cortijos* ("farmhouses") more than five kilometers from a school the government has created a special type of boarding school, *escuela hogar,* where the children live, study, and play, and where they remain until vacation time. Ninety-two of these schools have already been established throughout the country, many of them in Córdoba province where farms are predominant and towns distant. Some of the schools, such as the one for 130 boys in Granada, are private institutions and the state gives scholarships to the farm youths.

Life in the agricultural hamlets in recent years has been brightened for the young people by the establishment of Tele-Clubs. They get their

Dormitory of an escuela hogar, *a boarding school especially for farm boys in Granada*

name from the television sets given by the government through the Ministry of Information. Each Tele-Club receives a TV set and although this serves as a nucleus for the social and cultural life, the young members map their program of activities to suit themselves.

Some 2,500 of the Tele-Clubs now exist in Spain and each has 100 or more members, boys and girls. In some places the church auditorium is used as a meeting place; elsewhere, the town hall makes a room available. The ministry starts each Tele-Club off with a small library and the club adds to it on its own. Or a Tele-Club can buy books through the ministry on a 50-50 matching funds basis. The young people are interested in cultural matters and members of the nearest *Ateneo*—a private association of intellectuals which exists in all Spanish cities—often give lectures on art, music, and literature.

From time to time several Tele-Clubs in an area will arrange a day's meeting together. Not long ago Tele-Clubs from four neighboring villages in Seville province had a day-long get-together at one of the villages, Lora de Estepa, which has a population of 955. It started at mid-morning with an out-in-the-country swim in an *alberca,* a reservoir of irrigation water. Lunch for the 150 young men and women taking part was al fresco, with the fields serving as the picnic table and olive trees acting as parasols. Each of the young people brought his own food and exchanged it with one another—a bit of cooked ham for a slice of chicken, a banana for a few prunes, a chunk of beef for some canned mussels, and so forth. Almost everyone had a Spanish *tortilla* as a basic item for the picnic lunch and, although it was cold, they seemed to like it as much as if it had just come out of the frying-pan. The ministry sent along Coca-Cola and beer to top the lunch off. For two or three hours the boys and girls sang and danced in the fields, with guitars supplying their music.

The serious part of the day's program—the meeting—was scheduled for 5 p.m. (the start of the afternoon in Spain) in the Estepa cinema. The evening show was not to begin until 7:30 p.m. so the owner let the Tele-Clubs meet in his theater. It turned out the chief problem was a common one. The older people in the villages did not understand

Spanish banks often undertake various welfare projects in the cities. One program sends city children like these Málaga youngsters to mountain and seaside vacation camps

the purposes of the Tele-Clubs and what the young people did when they attended meetings. The problem was even more difficult for those young girls who happened to be elected an officer, or even president, of one of the clubs. In the small villages of Spain it is still the custom for the men to do everything. Girls reported at the assembly that they found it hard to explain to their parents why they were elected in preference to one of the young men. The meeting adjourned a little before 7 p.m. without any great decisions being made or programs mapped. All hoped that when they met again they would have progress to report in their difficulties with the "generation gap."

Social Welfare in the Cities

In the industrial city of Bilbao there is an unusual sign of extraordinary size. It is almost a block long, painted on the wall along the Nervión River, and just below the entrance to the Santander Railroad station. But what is really eye-catching is its message: "The Municipal Savings Bank of Bilbao performs the most extensive and beneficial social work in Vizcaya province."

Many people are surprised to see a city associated with a bank and even more surprised to learn that a bank is very active in social-welfare work. But neither is unusual in Spain. The Municipal Savings Bank of Bilbao was launched in 1907 with an investment by the municipality. The mayor is president and seven members of the city council are on the 12-member board, but the bank is operated like any other business. There are similar banking institutions throughout the country, even to extensive social-welfare programs. Savings banks in Spain, by law, must be operated as nonprofit enterprises, and all profits have to be channeled into projects that will benefit the community.

Some banks set up scholarships at universities and specialized schools. Others arrange music concerts and finance local symphonies. The Municipal Savings Bank of Bilbao has 26 projects on its list, and the list is being added to all the time. Current projects include 10 daytime *guarderias* which take care of 2,000 two-to-five-year-old children while their parents work; consulting clinics for children; a prenatal hospital; a residence for 14-to-23-year-old girls who have come to

The landing at Ayamonte, in the southwest corner of Spain, with Portugal on the far side across the Guadiana River. The only link between the two countries in the southern part of the Iberian peninsula is a small ferry boat which carries passengers and a few cars

Bilbao to work; three daytime centers for older people where they can read, play cards, and watch TV; and summer and year-round fresh-air vacation camps in the mountains and at the seaside for city-bred boys and girls. The people benefiting from the various welfare activities pay a little something because it makes them feel independent and, being Spaniards, they are too proud to accept anything that looks like hand-out. In 1967 the Bilbao bank's social-welfare budget was 38 million pesetas (about $550,000) and a budget of 43 million was planned for 1968.

Various barometers confirm that the diversified efforts to raise the standard of living of the Spanish people are having results. The people themselves like to measure progress with the automobile as a yardstick. At Valencia, 100 new cars go on the road daily, and the car population has risen in the past decade from 40,000 to 220,000. In Barcelona and Madrid, 300 new cars join the traffic every day. Economists point out that the First Economic and Social Development Plan, a four-year program that ended in December of 1967, aimed at raising personal income by 6 per cent and easily met that goal.

Portugal's Economy

Till recently, Portugal's economy was one of the fastest growing among the nations of western Europe, one reason being that it had started from a lower base than the others. Since 1953 there have been three development plans—two full-scale ones and a transitional one—and a new plan was started in January of 1968. Basically the plans set goals for investments in certain fields. Significantly, in a departure from the previous policy of the government, foreign investments are increasingly figuring in major projects. Oil discoveries in Angola and Mozambique will make Portugal self-sufficient; the important concession at Gabinda has been given to Gulf Oil Company.

Progress can be measured by the increased number of automobiles that appear daily, especially on city streets. On duty in Valencia is a sereno, one of Spain's typical nightwatchmen who open and close doors for residents from late evening to dawn

Tourism is the biggest single earner of foreign exchange. The tourism income, together with the remittances sent home by Portuguese who are working abroad—particularly in France and Germany—pays for the trade deficit and there is some left over for reserves. The Portuguese economy is still basically agricultural and nearly half of the land is cultivated.

Portugal has none of the investment income which United States bases now give Spain. Except for an agreement which grants the United States landing and certain other rights at a base in the Azores, and except for a handful of Americans on duty in Portugal as part of NATO, there is no U.S. military presence in the country. Portugal has enjoyed better relationships with the international community than its Iberian neighbor. Unlike Spain, Portugal was invited to join the Marshall Plan but she deliberately limited the amount and type of economic aid she drew from the American assistance program. Since 1954 Portugal has not received any economic grants from the United States and the only American aid she benefits from is the minuscule amount available from the surplus agricultural commodities program. Again unlike her neighbor, Portugal even belongs to NATO, which has kept the door shut on Spain.

Iberian Similarities and Differences

Portugal and Spain have many things in common, cultural heritage, the same peninsula as their home, and a big part of history. Their systems of government are also similar; but it would be wrong to exaggerate the similarities. A game could be played by two people, with one suggesting a point that Portugal and Spain have in common and the other responding by listing a difference. Both lists would be long, and it is hard to say which one would be exhausted first.

They both like music, but whereas the Spanish style is lively, loud, and generally merry, the Portuguese tends to be somber. The Portuguese *guitarra* is like a balalaika. It is heart-shaped, and has a dozen strings. Spain's guitar, as a Spanish caballero will point out quickly, is shaped like a woman. Portugal and Spain play the same type of football and each has a championship-grade team, but the ancient art of bullfighting is practiced in different ways, and neither likes the style used by the other. The Portuguese language is not at all a dialect of Spanish and the Portuguese resent any suggestion that it is. Persons with a Latin background, or a knowledge of French and Italian, can manage in Spanish, but they run into problems in Portuguese. Words in Portuguese often do not mean what it seems they should. The simple words on Portuguese doors for "Push" *(Empurre)* and "Pull" *(Puxe)* can be confusing.

If one enters a restaurant in Lisbon at 10 p.m. he might find the waiters eating because they are about to go home. If waiters in a Madrid restaurant were eating at ten in the evening it would be because they wanted to fortify themselves for several hours of work with the dinner crowd. Banks in Portugal keep morning and afternoon hours similar to those elsewhere in Europe, but in Spain after opening around 9 a.m. the banks remain open till 2 p.m.—and that is *it* for the day!

Church and State

Although both Portugal and Spain have Concordats with the Holy See, relations between Church and State are not at all alike in the two countries. The Church in Portugal is guaranteed, in the 1933 constitution, all the rights which it once enjoyed and which were either taken away or imperiled for almost two centuries. But the constitution provides specifically for the complete separation of Church and State, and there is no mention of God in it. Spain, on the other hand, makes clear at every possible opportunity—from the wording of the Concordat to the text of its laws—that it is Catholic, and that although other religions can now be practiced publicly, Roman Catholicism is the religion of the Spanish people. Article II of the Law on the Principles of the National Movement of May 17, 1958, says: "The Spanish nation regards as a badge of honor its respect for the Law of God, according to the doctrine of the Holy Catholic, Apostolic, and Roman Church, the one true and inseparable faith of the national conscience, which inspires the legislation of the country."

The Vatican's negative attitude toward colonialism rubs Portugal

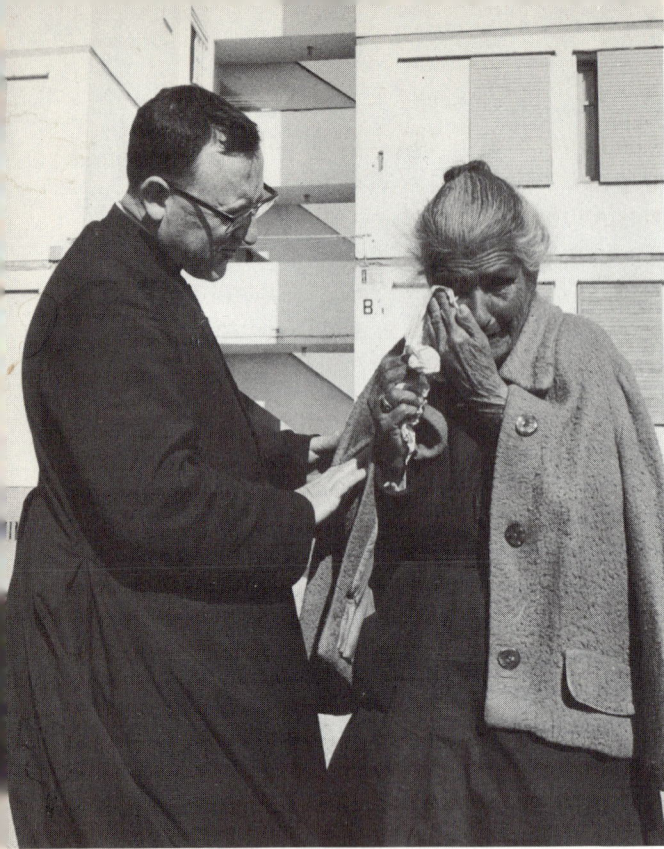

Social welfare must first be carried out on a personal level. In Málaga, a priest comforts an aged parishioner whose husband has recently died

the wrong way. Pope Paul VI's visit to the Eucharistic Congress in Bombay angered many in Portugal because the Portuguese possession of Goa had earlier been taken over by India. The Papal visit therefore was ignored in Portuguese newspapers. Yet, paradoxically, the Church of Portugal is sometimes accused of being too closely linked to the government, and this causes problems for both as there are supporters of the government which do not like the Church, and vice versa.

On the Spanish radio one can hear more religious programs than on the RAI network in Italy. Recitation of the Angelus and the saying of the rosary are daily events on many of the regional stations. This strong identification of the government with Catholicism does not give priests immunity from arrest in connection with labor disputes and separatist activities. The Concordat, farsightedly considering the possibility of priests being imprisoned, specified that when they were deprived of their liberty priests should be confined in religious houses or, at least, in places different from secular prisoners. This question came up in the summer of 1968 in the case of six Basque priests whose imprisonment was ordered. During their preliminary detention in Bilbao they were confined in houses normally used by families of prison personnel. Later they were transferred to the provincial prison of Zamora where similar arrangements were made for them that could satisfy both the verdict calling for their confinement and the wording of the Concordat.

Divorce is possible in Portugal under certain circumstances, but not in the case of people married in the Church. Spain does not permit divorce at all, and the only time it was possible was during the days of the Second Republic, just before the Civil War, when Church property was confiscated and the Jesuits, a Spanish-born society, were sent from the country.

There are differences likewise between the peoples of the countries themselves—between those from northern Portugal and those from south of the Tagus, between Andalusians and Galicians. The differences among the Spaniards are particularly pronounced. The 33 million Spaniards are so individualistic that it is sometimes said that Spain has 33 million dictators. All this makes it difficult to tell about the peoples of two countries in a single book, but encouragement comes from a famous Spaniard, Don Quixote, who said: "By a small sample we may judge of the whole piece."

Catalonia

Proud is an adjective often used to describe the Spanish. None are more proud of their heritage than the people of Catalonia. A poet has said that "even the fish in the Mediterranean wore the red and gold stripes of the kingdom led by Catalonia."

Why the red and gold stripes in Catalonia's coat-of-arms? There is a reason for everything and, in Spain, the explanation is usually a romantic one. In the case of the red and gold stripes it is said that after a battle against the Moors a count of Catalonia lay dying from a terrible wound in his chest. The king of France visited the battlefield to pay homage to the heroic count, and asked for his last wish. The count could not utter a word, but silently he placed his four fingers across the open wound near his heart. Then, he pressed the bloodied fingers against his resplendent shield. The resulting mark was adopted as Catalonia's coat-of-arms.

Catalonia is about the size of Belgium, but a great deal more mountainous. It is tucked into the northeast corner of the Iberian peninsula. There are four provinces: Lérida, Gerona, Tarragona, and Barcelona. Recently, in some of the geography books authorized for the schools, Lérida was missing from Catalonia, and showed up in the next-door region of Aragon. The textbook editors pointed out that the fruits and vegetables from the Lérida farmlands are the same as those produced along the Ebro in Aragon. But Catalonians argued that the human factor is more important than agricultural conditions, and that by language and tradition Lérida is Catalan. In future editions of the

The sardana *being performed in the square in front of the Barcelona cathedral*

textbooks Catalonia will be allowed to keep Lérida as one of its provinces!

Catalonia has the general shape of a right triangle, with the hypothenuse facing the Mediterranean on the east, its north side knifing through the Pyrenees and forming the Spanish-French border, and the western side flanking the region of Aragon. The upper part of Catalonia is dominated by the provinces of Lérida (in the northwest), Barcelona (at the center), and Gerona (in the northeast), while Tarragona spreads along the shoreline at the south. Lérida is the only province which does not open onto the sea. Two parallel lines of mountains, stemming from the Pyrenees, stretch southward through the central part of Catalonia, but the inland plains of Lérida provide plenty of room for farming. Agriculture plays a lesser role in the other provinces. A little over five million people live and work in the region, and most of them are concentrated in Barcelona province which is heavily industrialized. Catalans are known as industrious, intelligent, and highly civilized people. These human qualities, coupled with natural resources, make Catalonia one of Spain's wealthiest regions. The rivers and waterfalls pouring down from the Pyrenees are caught by a spectacular network of dams to make Catalonia rich in hydroelectric power. As a matter of fact, it exports power to neighboring France.

The Provinces

The soil of the Lérida farmlands is excellent because the area once was completely submerged, and is now coated with alluvial deposits left by the flowing water. The superb quality of the soil, backed up by an extensive irrigation system, makes the land highly productive. Fruit is a major crop. The pears are big and juicy, and sometimes weigh as much as a pound apiece. Truck trailers carry the produce daily to France and other parts of Europe.

Lérida's farmers own and work their own land, and are among the richest farmers in Spain. Their farms are not big, the average size being five acres, but the farmers have the machinery and modern equipment to farm the land, and the insecticides to protect it against disease.

A general view of one of the busiest harbors in Europe today, Barcelona

At harvest time students and people from the mountains pitch in. The pay is good because the crop has to be gathered quickly.

In Gerona the land is too mountainous for farming, but on the Emporda plain behind the mountains milk and beef cattle are raised. Coal, potassium, and salt mines are in the north of the province. Gerona's greatest asset is the 70 miles of coastline, between Blanes and the French border, known as the Costa Brava (the "Wild Coast"). It used to be known only to poets and painters, but tourists by the millions now throng the sand beaches of the Costa Brava each summer, and new hotels, apartment buildings, and camping sites are continuously cropping up along the Wild Coast. It is particularly wonderful to see the coastline from a boat. At times the sun showers the rocks with a bright redness; other times, with a soft pink or yellow. People who have seen the Costa Brava all their lives never get over its beauty. It is just the way one would hope it to be. The sand is golden, the water is deep blue, and the trees are very near to the sea.

The scarcity of rain and the lack of an irrigation system limits agricultural production in Catalonia's southernmost province of Tarragona. Near Tarragona city are acres of magnificent vineyards, and one of the grapes makes a champagne-type wine that is quite popular. The province also specializes in growing hazelnuts and almonds. In several recent seasons the hazelnut crop has been blighted by a baffling disease. A local farmer did some experimenting, and apparently discovered a way that will prevent the disease from striking again. Government technicians are double-checking the farmer's process. If it proves as effective as it seems, the clever farmer will get an official patent as well as the thanks of farmers everywhere. However, the province is becoming less agricultural and more industrialized all the time. Factories are anxious to move to Tarragona province because there is space, taxes are low, and the land is not expensive. Farmers can make more money selling their land than farming it. At Vandellos, a small village near Tarragona city, an atomic energy center for electricity is being built, using the French system as a model.

Potatoes are roasted for sale at an improvised outdoor stand in Barcelona

Small craft tied up along the Costa Brava, 70 miles of dramatic coastline between Blanes and the French border, and the site of sprouting hotels and apartments

From Barcelona city to Blanes at the boundary line of the province of Barcelona—40 miles to the north—underground streams feed wells, and there is a great deal of high-quality agricultural production. For example, Mataró is the shipping-point for carnations which are sold across Europe. (The 120-year-old Barcelona-Mataró rail line, by the way, was Spain's first railroad.) Another significant crop in the area north of Barcelona city is potatoes. They come to market earlier than potatoes elsewhere in Spain (with the possible exception of Valencia and the Canary Islands) so they bring the top prices. A variety of vegetables, from beans to asparagus, is grown along here too. Non-agricultural activity ranges from assembly plants for new cars to plants and factories producing chemicals, pharmaceuticals, paper, steel, and

55

heavy machinery. The area around Barcelona city is a busy textile center, producing cotton, wool, and synthetic fabrics that are sold not only in Spain but abroad, and a large leather industry is at Manresa. Barcelona city has so many big banks and insurance companies it would seem to be the world's financial hub. Barcelona city is both the capital of Barcelona province and of Catalonia, and is a captivating nucleus for northeastern Spain.

The City of Barcelona

Barcelona knows the problems that tumble into the life of a kindly old grandmother when distant relatives discover she has a comfortable house on a sunny seashore. The relatives who come to the city of Barcelona are from underdeveloped regions of Spain—Andalusia, especially. They come north for jobs and find work at better pay than they ever earned previously. The remain to build new homes and lives. The newcomers are happy because it is just as if they were living back home—except they are earning several times more. The per capita income in the Barcelona area is $1,000 a year, compared to $200 or $300 in Andalusia.

Barcelona is Spain's second largest city, but ranks first in commerce and is a pacesetter in many sectors of industry. For instance, she is responsible for two thirds of the national textile production. Furthermore, Barcelona is the biggest and busiest seaport on the Iberian peninsula. More than 1.7 million people now live in Barcelona, and inclusion of the suburbs boosts the figure to 2.5 million. The city's population has tripled since the beginning of the century, indicating what is ahead. By the start of the next century officials estimate that between 6.5 and 7.7 million people will be calling Barcelona their home.

People have been coming here since the days of the Iberians. One of history's most famous visitors was Christopher Columbus. On his return from America in 1493 he was royally welcomed in Barcelona by King Ferdinand and Queen Isabella. It was a happy time—Spain had just been united, and the Moors had finally called it quits. The royal couple still had not chosen a place for their capital and were holding court in a different city each year. The year that Columbus came back from America was Barcelona's turn.

A triumphant statue of Columbus tops a 75-foot pedestal at the Barcelona waterfront. If you could stand on the same lofty platform as the statue of Columbus you would get a splendid view of the old and the ever-new Barcelona.

As you look inland from your perch atop the Columbus monument, modern Barcelona has the appearance of a Greek amphitheater. Straight ahead, five miles away, is Mount Tibidabo, the main link in a mountain chain that rims the northwestern side of the city. It is only 1,700 feet high, and slopes gently toward downtown Barcelona and the sea. Flanking Barcelona are two rivers, the Llobregat on the southwest and the Besos on the northeast. New factories and housing projects for the workers are clustered along the banks of the rivers and it is there where Barcelona's industrial expansion is noticeable. The tree-lined Rambla which W. Somerset Maugham called the most beautiful street in the world leads from the Columbus monument toward Tibidabo, as if willing to meet the mountain half way. The Rambla follows the path of an old-time arroyo which haphazardly funneled mountain water to the sea. Midway between the Columbus monument and the Llobregat is an ancient hill, now within the city limits, the 575-foot-high Mont Juich. It is called the "Mountain of the Jews" because from the eleventh to fourteenth centuries its summit contained a Jewish cemetery, and many stones with Hebrew inscriptions have survived. (It is believed there were even older Jewish cemeteries in Barcelona than Mont Juich).

A few dozen yards from the monument to America's discoverer is the *Santa Maria*, a careful reproduction of Columbus's flagship, tied

The Columbus monument over-
looks the Barcelona waterfront

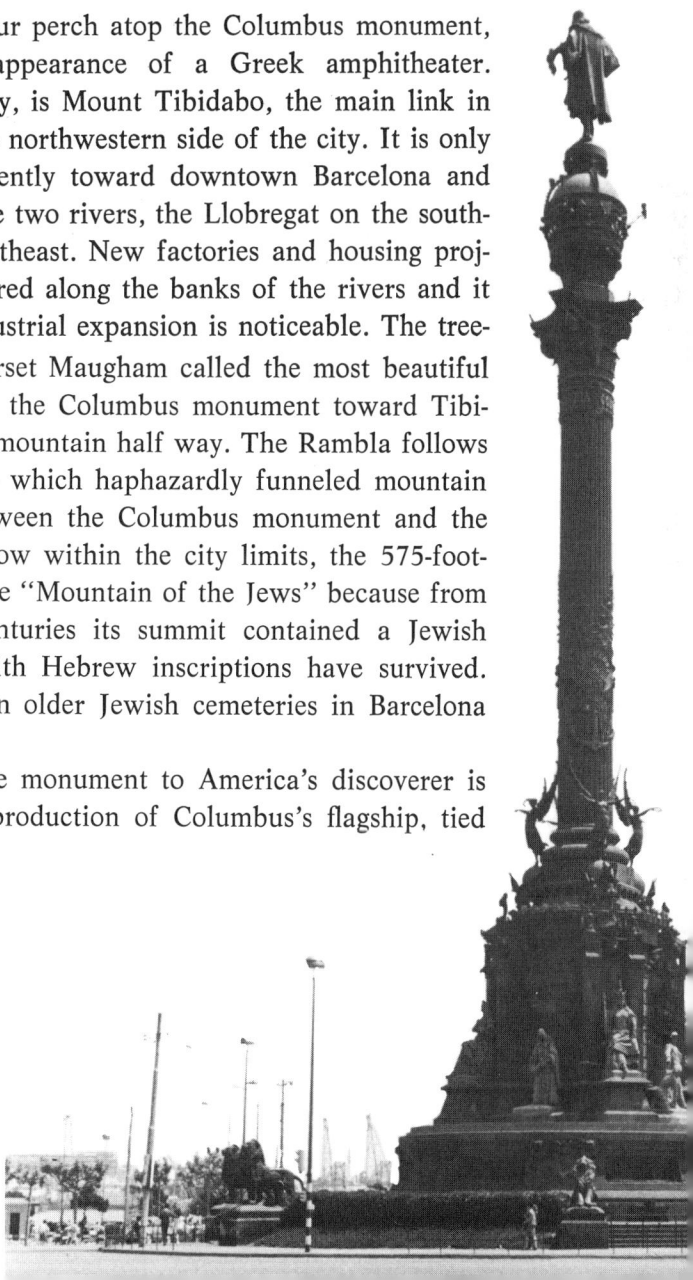

The Rambla appealed to both W. Somerset Maugham and this young artist, who paints the tree-lined street which runs from the waterfront to the center of Barcelona

up at the waterfront. It is so small it looks like a miniature model of the vessel that pioneered the Atlantic, rather than an exact copy. Not far from the *Santa Maria* is the pride of Barcelona, the Gothic quarter, built upon the remains of the old Roman city. Columbus on his arrival in Barcelona was received by the king and queen in their palace in the Gothic quarter and you can walk through the *Tinell*, the throne room, where the welcoming took place. For two centuries the *Tinell* had actually disappeared, even though it is about the size of a basketball court. A community of nuns had built a convent for themselves inside the huge room, and people forgot about the existence of the historic *Tinell*.

At the outbreak of the Civil War in 1936, the convent was wrecked and the nuns scattered. When the tumult subsided somewhat, city architects poking around the wreckage discovered the original walls and arched ceiling of the famous room of Christopher Columbus.

58

While the Civil War went on outside, restoration work was begun. If the military people knew what was going on, they would have drafted the workers into the army, but the restoration crew preferred what they were doing to fighting, and the civil authorities did not want the work to be stopped. So, although the restorers were working above ground, the restoration of the *Tinell* was carried out as an "underground" operation until the war ended.

Near the *Tinell* is the former royal chapel which is popular with today's young people for marriages. The staircases on either side of the chapel were needed by the king and queen so that they could descend from the palace into the chapel separately because the sexes used to be separated in church. Nowadays, Spanish men and women sit together in church, except for funerals.

Present-day sailors and other tourists examine the replica of the Santa Maria, *Columbus's flagship, now on permanent exhibit at the Barcelona waterfront*

Modern Barcelona

In Roman times Barcelona was indeed small. It fitted snugly within a defense wall less than a mile in circumference. In the thirteenth and fourteenth centuries, the wall was pushed out a bit further because the city had grown. But the great expansion of Barcelona did not take place until modern times. In fact, the city has grown so much that it cannot even be held in by the mountains and rivers which ring it. The rivers are about 10 miles apart, and the distance between waterfront and mountain chain is half that. This would seem to be plenty of room for a city, but it is not. Barcelona has one of the greatest population densities in the world.

On the top floor of Barcelona's City Hall, in a tiny office filled with charts, Xavier Subias has the facts and figures to prove this. Señor Subias is a husky, friendly man who is an architect-urbanist. On his desk are several American urbanism studies, such as the Committee for Economic Development's *Guiding Metropolitan Growth and Developing Metropolitan Transportation Policies.*

"In the downtown area," he will tell you," there are more than 1,000 persons working in each two and one half acres of space—plus 600 persons who permanently live there. On Manhattan Island, you have the same density of workers, but there is not the same number of fulltime residents."

The automobile is contributing to Barcelona's problems. There is now one car for every ten people. This is not a world record by any means, but as recently as 1953 Barcelona had only one car for every 70 persons. In 1960 the ratio was one car to 32 inhabitants. By 1980 it is expected there will be one car for every five Barcelonans.

In the summer of 1968 a large exhibit was staged to explain the city's growth problems to the citizens. Rather than have technicians tackle the problems in their offices and let the public know about them only when decisions had been made, Mayor José Maria de Porcioles y Colomer wanted to give the people a chance to participate. If they did not like what was being proposed—or, if they had a better idea—there was the opportunity to say so. This democratic concept is something new.

60

Easy-to-understand charts and diagrams showed how the city's growth required expansion of facilities. There were life-size models, too, of water purification units, sections of sewers big enough to walk through, and other material and equipment the city buys to keep Barcelona a nice place in which to live. All the different projects—from roads to sewers, from street-cleaning equipment to subways—had price tags on them. Exhibit-goers had a chance to study the city's income and decide how it was to be spent. Do we have enough money for more sewers? What about more school playgrounds? Can we afford to do everything? Are we willing to do more by paying more taxes? There were no easy answers to any of the questions raised by the exhibit. But the public participation in the decision-making gave assurance that the right solutions would be found.

One major project is to drill three tunnels through the mountain chain that faces the Columbus monument from across the city. The tunnels will really open up the behind-the-mountain area. The metropolitan development plan will then encourage the construction of office and government buildings, department stores, shopping centers, and modern high-rise housing units behind the mountains. Perhaps even the newly proposed second university for Barcelona will be located there.

Some residential building has already been taking place behind the mountains, but much of it is what urbanist Xavier Subias euphemistically calls "spontaneous urbanization." For example, a family from Andalusia will buy a small lot and build a house on it. The house will be just like the one they had back home—with whitewashed walls, bright flowers in tin cans on the window sill, and green plastic washtubs at the doorway. Some even erect in the dirt street an outdoor shrine to their favorite saint. Half of the original lot is sold to someone else to pay for the house. This family in turn proceeds to build a house to its own specifications. In these haphazardly developed areas on the fringes of Barcelona there are often no sewers, no sidewalks, no social facilities (schools, churches, and so forth). But what concerns authorities most of all is that unskilled workers are gravitating to these fringe areas.

In 1950, three fifths of the working people in Barcelona were unskilled. The figure has since shrunk to only 15 per cent—at the most, 20 per cent. But the majority of the settlers behind the mountains are unskilled workers, and their percentage keeps rising. A continuation of this trend could create a great social problem, separating one group of people from the other by barriers more formidable than mountains and rivers. Many reasons—traffic congestion, population density, preservation of the old Gothic quarter—have prompted municipal authorities to draft plans for revitalizing the outer area and moving the city's center toward it. But the human reason is there, too—a need to avoid social segregation.

The People and their Language

What are the people of Barcelona like?

Cosmopolitan, exuberant, cultured—these are some of the adjectives usually used to describe them. Most of all they are Mediterranean. This has nothing to do with their physical characteristics. They look pretty much like men and women, and boys and girls, in any metropolis. *Mediterranean* means they are open-hearted, warm, and instinctively friendly.

Here is an example. Mercè Arola is a Barcelona writer. One sunny afternoon we were walking through a patio of palm trees and singing birds in the Gothic quarter. A woman office-worker was seated near an open window, and Señorita Arola paused. Smilingly she said a few words to the woman inside the window. Later I asked if the woman was a friend. "No, not at all," Señorita replied, a bit surprised at my question. "Do I have to know her just to wish her a pleasant day?"

Mercedes (Mercè) is a favorite name for girls in Barcelona and it originates with the title for the city's patron, the Virgin of la Merced. Jorge (George) is a popular boys' name, and St. George is Catalonia's patron. *Mercedes* can be translated in several ways—"kindness," "grace," "mercy." Its popular use as a name began exactly 750 years ago after a dream of King James I of Aragon (the kings of Aragon were also Counts of Barcelona, and Barcelonans say the latter title was more important).

62

Young señoritas on the Rambla in Barcelona

During the time when Spain was being overrun by the Moors, Christian prisoners were taken to North Africa and held for ransom. One night, Barcelona people say, the Virgin appeared in a dream to King James I. She asked him to form an order of monks who would either exchange places with the prisoners or raise money to ransom them. King James I told the bishop the next morning about his dream, and learned he had experienced a similar apparition. They established the Ordin della Merced—the Order of Mercy. That was in 1218. The order still exists today, doing good works for the sick.

In Catalonia the names Mercedes and Jorge are also written as Mercè and Jordi, which are their equivalents in Catalan. The people of Catalonia speak two languages: Castilian, the official Spanish language; and Catalan, an old language of the region which was also used in parts of southern France. Like Castilian, Catalan comes from Latin. Señorita Arola uses Mercè instead of Mercedes. "I am Catalán, so my name should be that way," she says.

63

Final concert of the year's program of Juventudes Musicales Españolas, a branch of the international music organization for youth

The national government has frowned on widespread use of Catalan. Authorities in Madrid feel that Catalan could serve to divide the country at a time when unity is most needed. During the Civil War Catalonia was considered as being separatist-minded (that is, excessively desirous for a greater voice in its own affairs).

Before the war a dozen or more newspapers were published in Catalan. So far in the postwar period there are no Catalan-language newspapers. Only a few weekly reviews are permitted. Radio and TV in Catalonia are also exclusively in Castilian, except for a half-hour broadcast once a week and a few interviews and reports on secondary channels. Books can now be printed in Catalan, however. Last year, some five hundred titles in Catalan came off the presses. In the schools, Spanish is still the only language authorized. On bumpers of cars in Barcelona you can see *Català a l'Escola* stickers, urging classroom use of the Catalan language. In 1968 the national government in Madrid authorized after-class instruction in Catalan in the schools.

To bring the Catalan language to young people of Catalonia, a group of artists and writers a few years ago started a magazine for them, *Cavall Fort*. The magazine's name refers to a popular boys' game in Catalonia, literally translatable as "Strong Horse." *Cavall Fort* features the work of topflight writers in the Catalan language on history, mathematics, science, and other subjects of interest to young people. A recent issue, for instance, carried an illustrated vocabulary for a mountain trip—giving the names of plants, flowers, and animals you would come across in the higher altitudes of Catalonia. Joan Miro, the famous Catalan artist who celebrated his seventy-fifth birthday on the French Riviera in the summer of 1968, did one of the covers for the magazine as his contribution. *Cavall Fort* has won three Europe-wide "Best Cover" awards. Joan Miro's cover was one of the winners.

Catalan Music and Fiestas

Music is a traditional part of Barcelona life and the young people are now studying it so that they can enjoy it more. Juventudes Musicales Españolas, a branch of the international music organization for youth, was started in Barcelona in 1952 and 14,000 boys and girls from 125 schools in the city, plus 6,000 students from the rest of Catalonia, participate in its program. Banks and local governments are among the benefactors. Once a month students in groups attend a concert in the Palacio de la Música. An admission fee of 15 pesetas (20 cents) is charged to teach the youngsters that concerts have to be paid for, but if a school says this is too high for their students a lower amount is charged. The office of Manuel Capdevila, secretary-general of Juventudes Musicales Españolas, literally tinkles at concert time each month as school directors bring him jars, boxes, and other containers crammed with small-denomination coins. The youngsters are in the 8-to-14 age group, but a special program is arranged for those 14 to 16 years old.

The monthly concert series climaxes with an exciting finale when all the participating students in Barcelona are invited to a musical get-together in the prestigious main hall of the Palacio Nacional, and diplomas are ceremoniously awarded to the schools which have been active in the program during the year. A convention was booked into the Palacio Nacional at finale time in 1968 and the young people's concert had to be shifted to the Sports Palace. The acoustics were bad, but the day was a success. Six thousand youngsters jammed the stands of the immense sports hall and even the bleachers near the ceiling were filled. The children from each school wore their regular uniforms—berets, jackets, white blouses, and so forth—the outfits varying from school to school. Each section of the young audience by the way they were dressed contributed to a giant patchwork of color, and the variety added a delightful note to the concert.

Before Antoni Ros Marra raised his baton to direct the Municipal Orchestra of Barcelona in its first number the president of Juventudes Musicales Españolas, Dr. Jordi Roch, explained the function of each instrument. He also exhorted the youngsters not to move their lips *or* their programs while the orchestra played. "The whole body must listen," he explained. The boys and girls did better on keeping silent than the average audience of adults. The 45-minute concert consisted primarily of a 13-part work called *Variations*, and the immense scoreboard which normally tallies basketball, hockey, and other scores indicated the number of the sequence that was being played. Each sequence featured a particular group of instruments, the trumpet section making the biggest hit.

Catalans like to sing and the 45-minute concert was followed by singing guided by Ordol Martobell, director of the adult *Coral Sant Jordi*. They first warmed up with a Catalan song which is sung in various voice ranges and is appropriately called, "Let Us All Sing Happily Together." They concluded with "How Wonderful It Will Be When Everyone Loves One Another." It was a song they had learned during the year, and they seemed to know it well.

Students at the Costa y Llobera school in Barcelona join in a round of songs

There are many singing groups among the boys and girls of Catalonia. (The *Coral Sant Jordi* has a young people's singing group called *Esquitx*, which means "Splash.") In the spring of 1968, two thousand Catalan boys and girls from 9 to 16 journeyed to Lérida city for a one-day songfest. It was the second *trobada* for young people of Catalonia and bigger than the inaugural one at Manresa the year before, when 800 boys and girls gathered for a day of song. At Lérida city the young people sang in the main square for the townspeople, and then visited local hospitals and asylums to sing some more. The annual song-fest is not a singing contest but only a means for the young people to meet and to sing. It is not necessary to have a great voice to join in the singing. The only qualification is a *desire* to sing.

Mediterranean people know that life is not always easy for everyone. So they try to brighten everyday life all year long with flowers, birds, and kind words—simple, easy-to-do things. But they really shine at fiesta time! The biggest festival honors the Virgin of la Merced. It starts at the end of September, and lasts a month. A thick book lists all the goings-on. There are outdoor and indoor events, concerts in the park, street dancing and singing—fun in general. The amusement parks on Mont Juich and on Tibidabo are packed. Young Tyrolean musicians in black felt hats and well-worn lederhosen journey to Barcelona from Innsbruck. Drum majorettes, outfitted like American high-school cheerleaders, lead bands from southern France. A topnotch event is the Mediterranean Song Fest in which groups from as far off as Israel compete.

St. George is not forgotten, either. His day comes on April 23. There are two festivals this day—The Rose and The Book. Roses are everywhere; men give roses to the ladies; it is a lover's day. However, the anniversaries of the deaths of Cervantes and of Shakespeare are celebrated the same day, so everyone gives a book along with a rose. On that day bookstores are allowed to set up stands on the sidewalks, and books are sold at reduced prices. It is a happy way to welcome spring.

Throughout Catalonia people like to sing and dance, and in every town there are fiestas which match in spirit, if not in size, those of Barcelona.

Prominent figures at fiesta time are the Giants. Every Catalán city, from Barcelona to the smallest place in the Pyrenees, has its favorite pair who take to the streets when there is something to celebrate. The Giants apparently originated with the medieval custom of public processions featuring biblical figures. David slaying the Philistine giant Goliath with a sling was a favorite, and the liking of the people for the David and Goliath story might be the reason that the Giants have survived the passing of the old-time processions.

The Giants and their towering companions are not the same as they used to be. In the transformation from medieval to modern times the giant was paired with a tall female companion. The Giants of Barcelona are dressed like a medieval king and queen. Elsewhere, they are warriors, aristocrats, farmers, or gypsies. There is no set rule; imagination is the only limit. When the Giants strut through the streets to the tune of lively music—sometimes dancing and pirouetting—spectators toss coins for their maintenance and for the pay of the unseen men that carry them.

Esteban Bassols, a senior Barcelona city official, likes to muse about a meeting of all the Giants of Catalonia at a Festival of la Merced in the '20s. "Dozens and dozens of these big, beloved figures were on hand," according to Señor Bassols, "and the old people say that the parade was fabulous that year."

Catalonia's national dance is the *sardana*. In parks and village squares throughout Catalonia the *sardana* is still danced on Sundays. The square in front of Barcelona's cathedral is a dance-floor each Sunday at noon and each Wednesday evening at 7:30 o'clock.

Sometimes several hundred dancers gather in front of the Barcelona cathedral for the *sardana*, most of them are young men and women. The dancers form into circles, holding hands. Usually a circle is made by a dozen persons, but it can be much bigger. An orchestra featuring trombones and trumpets helps everyone keep in step, and one member of each circle (usually a girl) acts as the dance director, warning those dancing with her to watch their step for a sudden change in the rhythm. There are short steps and long ones. The *sardana* is a very ceremonial and almost formal type of dance, but it is much fun. Young Barcelonans obviously like it. Sometimes on a Wednesday evening, just as the dancing is going well, a thundershower scatters everyone, and the cathedral square suddenly takes on the appearance of a deserted stage set. An hour later, when the rain stops, almost all the dancers rush back to the square to take up the *sardana* where they left off.

The poet Maragall once described the *sardana* as being the "dance of a people which goes forward hand in hand."

The people of Catalonia are indeed going forward. One sees that in the way they live, work, and face life.

Andalusia

On a sunny day in May in 1829 Washington Irving and a Russian diplomat set off on horseback across Andalusia. Their journey began in the elegant metropolis of Seville, wound through the narrow, flowered streets of Córdoba, and climaxed on the heights of Granada, the magic city of poetry, gypsies, and Moorish legends. The celebrated New Yorker who "knew" Ichabod Crane and the legendary people of Sleepy Hollow also found storybook figures on the Spanish side of the Atlantic, and told about them in his *Tales of the Alhambra*. Andalusia is a remarkable, particularly beautiful section of Spain that brims over with romance and history.

Andalusia stretches across the whole southern part of Spain, and occupies a sixth of the Spanish mainland. The side west of Gibraltar —the side bordering Portugal—faces the Atlantic, and the rest of Andalusia fronts on the Mediterranean. The Romans called Andalusia Baetica; the Vandals, one of the Germanic tribes which arrived in Spain after the Romans, probably gave the region its present name; and the Moors, the most recent of the invaders and those who stayed the longest, left the most visible marks.

Moorish customs have especially lingered in the villages. Houses are bunched together on a hillside along narrow, winding lanes—determined to prevent the sun's rays from touching the ground or from entering inside. Houses in Andalusia are a vivid white. It would seem as if a giant bucket of white paint had spilled down a sun-bleached hill. The blinding whiteness of everything is accented by the stern

A Granada resident follows a little-used but old trail which skirts one side of the Alhambra. In the background is the Albaicin quarter of the city

brightness of the sun. The only black one sees, poet Manuel Machado has observed, are the eyes of the women.

Long after the Moorish occupation came to an end women of Andalusia continued to wear veils. Even as recently as the late 1940s women covered their faces in such widely separated Andalusian towns as Vejer de la Frontera, in Cádiz province, and Mojácar on the eastern coast. They were called Las Tapadas—"the Hidden Ones." These were just not old women, either, for young girls in their late teens were also among "the Hidden Ones."

The Moors, too, are remembered in the everyday language. Alcázar was originally a Moorish word for the monumental fortresses that one still sees in the chief cities of Andalusia. Many Spanish words beginning with "al" have a Moorish origin. Names of Andalusia's rivers also hint that they were known by the Moors. The Guadiana, for instance, separates Andalusia from Portugal. The prefix "guadi" or "guada" comes from the Arab word *wadi* which is associated with water. The Arabs never had seen so much fresh water until they reached Andalusia.

A row of cottages, with flowered balconies and television aerials, on the southern Spanish coast of Málaga, the birthplace of Picasso

Málaga is a busy seaport, and this outdoor vendor's stand is designed to appeal to sea-minded customers in the downtown area

Don Eduardo Fajardo, the director of the Granada daily newspaper *Patria*, describes Granada as a "city of the spirit," pointing out that painters, poets, and musicians have always felt at home there. The same can be said about Andalusia itself. Every province has some native son—or an adopted one—who has helped to show the world that this is indeed a Region of the Spirit. Cádiz was the birthplace of composer Carmen de Manuel de Falla. Pablo Picasso was born in Málaga.

In this land where there are many donkeys, the most famous is the one depicted by the late Nobel prize winner for literature, Juan Ramón Jiménez in his *Platero y Yo*. Often as you wander through Andalusia you will be reminded of the Seville poet, Gustavo Adolfo Becquer. He

73

was known for his poems but his legends are filled with romance. One legend deals with the statue of a handsome cavalier leaning over on a moonlit evening to kiss a bewitching lady statue in the garden beside him. Statues in the still gardens of Andalusia encourage the feeling that maybe there was some truth to the poet's story.

Agriculture is the backbone of Andalusia. Wheat, grapes, cotton, and citrus fruit, as well as fighting bulls, are grown. But the main product is the olive. Many folk songs have been written about olive growing, and harvest time hums with old melodies sung by young people. At Algeciras in Cádiz province ferries link Spain with north Africa, and there are important international seaports at Málaga, Huelva, and, fifty miles from the sea, at Seville (which is Spain's only inland port). As is generally the case throughout Spain, the Andalusian provinces have capitals with the same names. There are eight provinces in Andalusia, and two distinct zones—one lying along the Guadalquivir Valley, and the other along the Mediterranean. The valley includes four provinces (Seville, Córdoba, Jaén, and Huelva) and part of a fifth, Cádiz. The Mediterranean zone consists of the provinces of Málaga, Granada, and Almeria, and the eastern part of Cádiz province. Cádiz has the greatest population density of any of the provinces, and Almeria is the least populated.

The Guadalquivir Valley

Two thirds of the eight million people of Andalusia live along the Guadalquivir Valley. The largest province is Seville, with a population of 1.2 million. The city of Seville itself accounts for half of the province's population. Córdoba, the next largest city in the valley, has 200,000 inhabitants.

The Guadalquivir, Andalusia's most famous river, rises in the mountains at the east end of the region and flows through both Córdoba and Seville on its way to the Atlantic at the west. The Guadalquivir Valley is shaped like a triangle. Two sides are bordered by mountain chains running more or less east and west, and the third side fronts the low, sandy coastline of the Atlantic. Andalusia's main reserve of forests is packed among the sierras at the eastern part of the valley, and it is a wild area where deer, boar, and eagles make their home, confident that the chance of intruders is slight. Despite the rugged surroundings and ferocious neighbors, delicate butterflies of species unknown elsewhere in the world also live here in apparent contentment. Except among the sierras of Jaén province, the winters are relatively mild. Summertime is something else. The section between Seville and Córdoba is generally at the top of the list when Spain's summertime high temperatures are reported and is called "the Frying Pan of Spain." The main growing area in Spain for olives is at Martos in Jaén province; and at the western end of the valley in Cádiz province sherry wines are produced in the town of Jerez. From the port of Huelva city, west of Cádiz, Columbus set sail. Rich mining deposits are often just below the surface of what looks like empty, barren land. Olive groves and lead mines are side by side, for instance, in Jaén. In biblical times King Solomon used to send his ships from the other end of the Mediterranean to Huelva to load cargoes of copper and other metals from the province's extraordinary mines.

In the dry season the water in the Guadalquivir is so low that cattle graze on grass and shrubs in the river bed. People of Córdoba, cut off from the sea, use the Guadalquivir as a swimming pool. Families pack

The Guadalquivir serves as a swimming pool for residents of Córdoba on a hot day

a lunch and seek out a patch of river bed as a picnic ground. It is amusing to see large black umbrellas opened on the river bed like ominous storm signals on a bright sunny day. But Cordovans know that the same umbrella that is welcome in a winter rain can be just as useful on a burning day in July. With great dignity the woman of the family lays out the picnic lunch on a white cloth brought from home. The menu depends on the tastes and the financial circumstances of the family but the Andalusian specialty, *gazpacho,* is always present. From an old wine bottle she pours into plastic cups a broth, fortified with olive oil and vinegar, which is the base of *gazpacho.* Then, from small containers which she magically produces from an old canvas airline bag the woman sprinkles diced onions, peppers, carrots, and other vegetables into the cups of soup. At the center of the cloth she places a plate of olives, and her family dip into them as if they were peanuts. Large tomatoes are passed around and eaten like apples. Slices are carved from a cold leg of lamb for sandwiches which she carefully makes herself, using a heavily crusted homemade bread that is made only with water, salt, yeast, and flour. Oranges are usually the dessert, but sometimes there is homemade gingerbread, too. Throughout the meal a local wine that costs about 10 pesetas a quart is drunk, but no one drinks very much. A quart will be enough for a husband and wife and two or three children. The mother of a family drinks less wine than her husband, and the children drink less than she does. But all have some wine during the meal. Even a toddler is offered a few sips.

Across the Puente Nuevo—on the south side of the Guadalquivir—a new residential area is being developed, and six-story modern apartment houses have been built. There is one apartment to a floor, and each unit has three or four rooms, in addition to a kitchen and bath. The apartments are sold from 200,000 to 300,000 pesetas depending on size and location. The higher-priced ones have a fine view of the river and of the old part of town.

Let us look at the capitals of Seville and Córdoba provinces which were two of the three main cities on the Andalusian itinerary of Washington Irving.

Chess is a popular game in Spain and here in an outdoor café in Granada, it is being played with appropriate concentration

Seville

The city of Seville has received so many compliments across the centuries that it is something like a lovely girl who is aware of her blessings. Some say it is the most beautiful city in Spain. A sixteenth-century poet, Fernando de Herrera, called Seville "Queen of the Ocean." To others it is the best bullfighting area in the country. Most of the great bullfighters have come from Andalusia, and many of them were born in a poor district of Seville called Macarena. Bullfighters traditionally pray to an image known as La Macarena ("Our Lady of Hope") before stepping into the ring to face a wild bull.

Seville's cathedral contains the tomb of Christopher Columbus and stands on the site of the Great Mosque where Moslems prayed when

The cathedral at Seville, with its celebrated tower, La Giralda, once a minaret during the Moorish occupation

the city was part of the Moorish kingdom. The immense Patio of the Orange-Trees is the courtyard in which Moslem worshipers used to perform their ablutions before entering the Great Mosque. The most spectacular relic is the Giralda Tower, which was the minaret from which Moslems were summoned to prayer. It is Seville's most outstanding landmark. When the cathedral was built in the fifteenth century, the Moslem minaret was topped by a bell-tower. Most square-shaped church towers seen in Andalusia nowadays top former mosques. From the top of the Giralda Tower one can see, on the outskirts of Seville, the remains of the old Roman city where the emperors Trajan and Hadrian were born. (Marcus Aurelius and Theodosius were also born in Spain.) Clustered in the ruins are what is left of the largest Roman theater in all of Spain.

Holy Week at Seville, when huge silver-encrusted images and

tableaus are carried through narrow, twisting streets on the backs of men, is Spain's outstanding religious fiesta—and perhaps the world's. There are eight processions in Holy Week (two on Good Friday—dawn and evening). The night before one procession city employes cover the streets with wild ferns. Under the feet of the marchers the following morning the ferns exude a fragrance of mint that permeates the atmosphere. The procession takes place after services in the cathedral, and during it throbbing songs called *saetas* are sung by people from house balconies in a salute to a religious image (such as The Virgin of la Macarena) as it is carried through the streets. The melody of a *saeta* has a lamentful, Moorish tone and its words are gracefully phrased, sounding as if they might have been written by a Moorish poet of Seville many centuries ago. "Thy face glows with a beauty possessed by no other woman in the world," is the type of *saeta* sung to the Virgin.

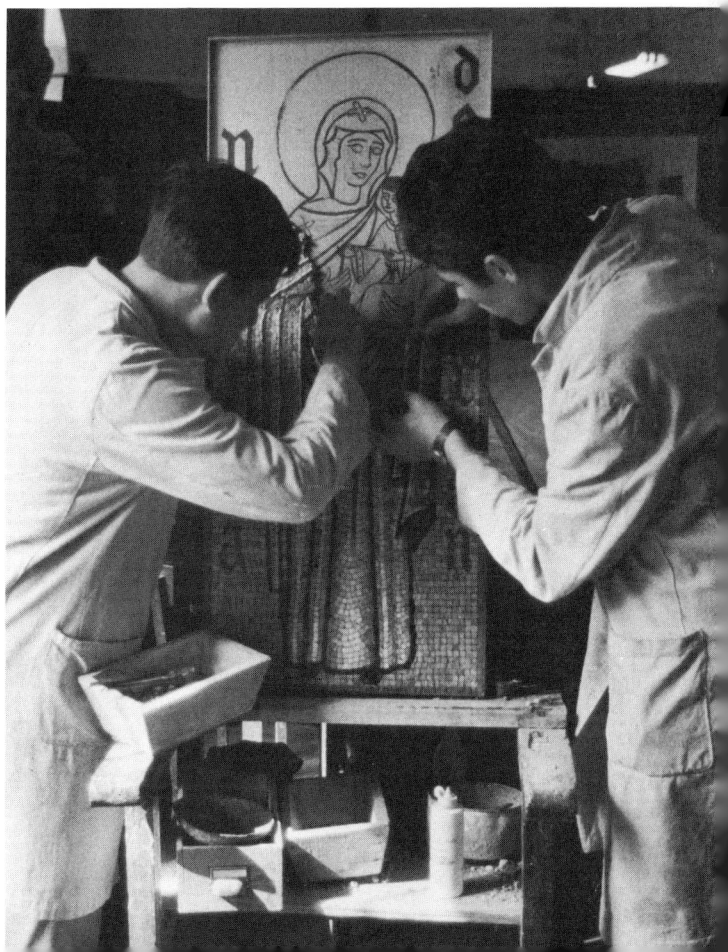

The beauty of Spanish religious art is known throughout the world. Here tile workers in the monastery of Puig, north of Valencia, repair a mosaic

A number of times a year the Seville cathedral, which ranks in size after St. Peter's in Rome and St. Paul's in London, is the scene of an unusual form of liturgy. Ten choir boys, decked out in flouncy silk costumes of brilliant colors and wearing wide-brimmed hats with perky plumes, dance before the altar and keep time by clicking castanets. It is a solemn dance, done in measured steps, on such feasts as Corpus Christi and the Immaculate Conception. These extraordinary young dancers are called "Los Seises"—"The Six-Year-Olds" but they are really closer to ten or eleven. A long time ago, according to the story, word reached Rome about the dancing and the castanet-playing during solemn cathedral services and the Pope declared that it seemed to be altogether sacrilegious. The people of Seville replied that it was a liturgical dance of homage to God, and had always been performed. Judiciously the Pope decided that they could keep doing what they had been doing until the costumes of "Los Seises" wore out. Thus, very special care is given to these sixteenth-century garments.

On the right bank of the Guadalquivir, just across the Isabella II bridge, is Seville's smallest street. It is in the Triana quarter, a famous center of tile-makers, and is more of an alley than a street, being probably not even 50 feet long and 5 feet wide. No one uses it any more. A locked gate bars the entrance at one end and a gloomy archway frames the ruins of a broken-down building at the end near the Guadalquivir. The passageway itself is as cluttered as an abandoned junkyard, with chunks of wood, stone, and molding odds and ends thrown every which way. What makes one take notice of the street is its name, Callejón de la Inquisición. One would almost think that the debris was a deliberate act of symbolism. In the beautiful setting of Seville the name of this ugly little street abruptly calls to mind the Inquisition. That was an unhappy period in Spanish history when misguided Christians persecuted people only because they did not share the same religious beliefs. The Inquisition operated throughout Europe, but it started in Spain.

The spiritual fire kindled by the Crusades and the urge to drive the "infidel" from their homeland got out of human control at the very moment when Spain had at last subdued the Moors and Spaniards were looking beyond the peninsula for new worlds to conquer. The glory year of 1492 was stained by the Catholic monarchs themselves, Ferdinand and Isabella, when they issued the decree expelling the Jews from Spain.

Córdoba

Modern Spain has been trying to make amends for the wrongs done by Spaniards to other Spaniards centuries ago. Córdoba was the capital of Moslem Spain from the eighth to the eleventh century and was the most populous city in Europe—over one million inhabitants. The population has shrunk to about a fifth of what it was and the eighth-century Mezquita, the Great Mosque with countless peppermintstick-colored columns supporting the horseshoe-shaped arches of the nineteen naves, is now both a museum and a site of Christian worship. Two hundred yards away the word "Judios" is written in large letters on a white-washed street wall, a quiet reminder that in the days of Córdoba's greatness this was the Jewish quarter of the city. No Jews live in

An ancient waterwheel used by the Moors now lies idle on the banks of the Guadalquivir

Córdoba nowadays and in all of Spain there are not more than 6,000. But Spain's new religious liberty law makes it legal to practice Judaism (and other religions) openly. This might encourage the return home of descendants of the ancient Sephardim—the Spanish Jews so called because of the biblical name, "Sefarad," for Spain.

Córdoba now proudly honors a Jewish citizen of long ago, Maimonides, who was a philosopher and physician as well as a rabbi. The tiny Plaza de Tiberiades in the one-time Jewish quarter contains a statue of Maimonides which shows him seated, looking solemn yet strikingly humane and simpático. The inscription says simply: "Córdoba to Maimonides." The statue is dated according both to the Hebrew calendar (5724) and the Christian one (1964). A few doors down the street is Córdoba's old synagogue, built in 1315, and now a national monument. Although left in enforced idleness for centuries this holy place retains the warmth and friendly intimacy that nourished it when the Jews of Córdoba used it as a place of prayer to God. Plaques

A statue of Maimonides, Jewish scholar and citizen of twelfth-century Córdoba

Bullfight fans line up to buy tickets for a corrida in Granada. The "Sol" sign indicates that only cheaper priced tickets—those in the sun—are sold at this window. Tickets for the shady side of the arena are sold at the "Sombra" window

in its flowered patio contain tributes to Maimonides from the government of Spain and from Córdoba, made on March 30, 1935, the eighth centenary of his birth.

One tribute reads: "Córdoba, his homeland, offers him the veneration of her memory."

The companion tribute says: "Spain, his nation, expresses her homage to the immortal genius of Judaism."

The square at the beginning of the Jewish quarter is named after Maimonides, and one of its buildings houses the city's Bullfighting Museum. To some foreigners bullfighting, perhaps, is a sport but in Spain it is an art. It is a ballet of death—a symbol of Spain's perennial fight against poverty and death. And as Hemingway pointed out it is the only art in which the artist is in danger of death and in which the brilliance of the performance is left to the fighter's honor. In the

83

museum capes, posters, and a thousand-and-one things associated with bulls and matadors are preserved with all the dignity worthy of objects of art.

Manuel Rodriguez Sanchez, generally rated as the best bullfighter of modern times, was also born in Córdoba and a memorial plaque is on the wall of his birthplace, a two-story white-framed house in the Calle Torres Cabrera. He was known better as Manolete, the diminutive form of his name Manuel. Manolete met his death at the traditional *five o'clock* in the afternoon of August 28, 1947, in a *corrida* at Linares in the province of Jaén. In cafés and restaurants in Córdoba, and elsewhere in Andalusia, Manolete's gaunt, serious face stares from a photo on the wall. No name is on such photos. None is needed. A huge rectangular scar marks his left cheek. Manolete received that wound in the 1944-45 *temporada* ("season") at Valencia. Even in moments of happy triumph Manolete looked serious. An Englishwoman is said to have once asked Manolete why he was always so serious. Solemnly he replied: "Madam, the bull is always serious."

Córdoba has had many famous sons in all periods of its history. The Roman philosopher Seneca was born here. More than a dozen centuries after the Roman occupation, Córdoba was the birthplace of Fernandez Gonzalo, known as El Gran Capitan. That would be equivalent to commander-in-chief or five-star-general today. El Gran Capitan led the Spaniards to their battles at Naples, Calabria, and other points on the Italian peninsula. An inscription on the statue erected on the 500th anniversary of his birth in 1953 tells what kind of a man he was. It says: "I would much prefer going forward two steps, even if it would mean death, than living one hundred years if it meant taking a step backward."

The face of the statue is unmistakably Cordovan, local people say, adding that the death mask of "Lagartijo," a celebrated nineteenth-century bullfighter from Córdoba, was used as the model.

The Mountains and Vegas

The other zone of Andalusia lies to the southeast of the Guadalquivir Valley, and is about one third its size. Mountains reach down to the

84

Mediterranean, and the shoreline is laced with sandy coves and bays. In the Sierra Nevada of Granada province is 11,477-foot Mount Mulhacén, the highest mountain on the Iberian peninsula. At its base is Trevélez, the highest village in Spain. A road leads from the city of Granada to the top of the Sierra Nevada. No highway in Europe tops it. From this lofty viewpoint one can look upon the inviting beaches of the Mediterranean, the Costa del Sol. In the high back-country winter temperatures can be quite cold, but along the coast winter weather never makes anyone shiver. Summers are dry and warm, and temperatures climb when the *terral* wind blows from North Africa. It is unmistakably a tropical atmosphere. This is the land of sugar cane, bananas, figs, pineapples, and almonds. It is the only place in Europe where tropical plants can be cultivated. Spread among the mountains are three wide, productive plains called vegas. The vega near Granada city is irrigated by waters from the Genil River. Some of the farms in the Gaudix and Baeza Vegas, in the northeastern part of the province, are very large—of as much as 100,000 acres. Vast ownership of this type is known as a *latifundio*. Workers hired to cultivate the land generally live with their families in a *finca* ("ranch-house") on the property. The official minimum wage is 100 pesetas a day but some workers earn between 200 and 250. On the southern side of the Sierra Nevada, along the Alpujarra slopes, is the completely opposite type of farm, a *minifundio,* just large enough for a family to work and live on.

Granada

Washington Irving, on arriving at Granada, had the good fortune of being permitted to reside for several months in the Alhambra, the last Moorish stronghold in Spain. Visitors today would not be so fortunate. Not that there is lack of room on the grounds and in the galaxy of palaces which comprise this Wonder of the World. At the end of the fifteenth century it housed 40,000 people when the Moors were making a last stand to defend their steadily shrinking kingdom against the Christian armies. The Alhambra is now a museum, and although visitors cannot use it as a hotel they can wander through its gardens, climb its towers, and linger by the fountains which were known to the people

Young residents of the Albaicin quarter in Granada. In the immediate background is the Alhambra and behind it is the ever-white Sierra Nevada

Washington Irving wrote about. The Moors loved water and, bringing it from the mountains by aqueducts, they funneled it to the alabaster-lined baths and to the fish ponds, ornamental fountains, and basins, and to the cascades with which they adorned courts and gardens. The Moors were driven out of Baeza, 60 miles northeast of Granada city, in 1227 and they first set up temporary headquarters for their kingdom in the Albaicin district of Granada while the Alhambra was being built.

Nearly 6,500 people now live in the Albaicin district which is a mile from the center of Granada and which fills a low hill on the opposite side of the Darro River from the Alhambra. The Albaicin district retains a Moorish look. Many of the small white houses have gardens called *cármenes*. Streets are narrow, winding, and steep. Food shops are tiny cubicles nestled inconspicuously among the one- and two-story buildings. In the afternoon the village looks deserted because everyone is hiding from the sun. Curling up another hill at the foot of the Albaicin district is a road leading to Sacromonte, the "Holy Mountain." The road is only a mile long, but it is steep. It is said that seven disciples of St. Peter journeyed here in the first century to evangelize the land. One of them, St. Cecilio, was martyred and buried alive in a grotto on the mountain. It soon acquired the name of Holy Mountain, and for centuries monks have been living on Sacromonte.

Granada's celebrated community of gypsies helped make Sacromonte known with their singing and dancing. For years the 2,000 gypsies of Sacromonte lived in 200 caves dug in the mountain. The gypsy life was not anywhere as romantic or carefree as it sounds in song and story.

A canvas awning is hung above the main street of Granada to shield passers-by from the strong noonday sun

A survey published in 1963 disclosed that no more than a dozen of the 200 caves could be considered comfortable. These were the only ones equipped with such conveniences as electricity and telephone. That turned out to be a bad year, coincidentally, for the gypsies of Granada. For two months in the winter of 1963 rains steadily drenched Granada and many of the gypsy caves collapsed, even burying some gypsies alive. Since then, almost all the gypsies have moved from Sacromonte to makeshift dwellings in the La Chana *barrio* on the other side of town. Conditions are even worse for them in their new homes. It is a flatland and the summer heat scorches the wooden shelters of the gypsies. For all their drawbacks the caves on Sacromonte were at least cool in summer, and about 200 gypsies still live there.

Teaching Gypsies

The elementary school at the side of the road on Sacromonte observed its eightieth anniversary in 1968. This is not necessarily old for a school but the one on Sacromonte was unusual when founded in 1888

Youngsters in Granada's gypsy quarter examine a large topographical map of Spain on the ground of the school yard at the pioneering Escuela del Ave Maria. The map helps students learn geography in a learn-by-playing system

and it still is out of the ordinary. The method of teaching, a pioneering system of learn-by-playing, was specifically designed for restless children, such as gypsies, whose attention it is hard to get and to keep. The school yard is marked off for special games. One end, for instance, is covered with a huge topographic map showing the mountains, rivers, and other surface features of the Iberian peninsula, and the boundary lines of provinces and principal cities. Students make imaginary trips through the peninsula, determining which journey involves crossing the largest (or smallest) number of rivers; or the most (or fewest) mountains; or the least (or greatest) number of provinces; and so forth. Miniatures of foods, raw materials, and other products of each province are stacked within its boundaries, and this suggests additional games. "Let's make a paella," a teacher proposes. "Where do we have to go to get the ingredients?" One after the other students answer: Valencia for the rice; Jaén for the oil; Cáceres for meat; Zamora for wheat; La Coruña for fish. After all possible ingredients for a paella are exhausted —as well as their sources—someone might say that Vizcaya can provide the metal for the baking pan. That will prompt another youngster to say that coal can be obtained in Asturias. And so on. History and other subjects are taught in similar ways. But the main thing students learn is that the making of even a simple dish like a paella requires the efforts and cooperation of Spaniards in various parts of the country.

The school was founded by Don Andrés Manjón, a teacher who became a priest at the age of 40. He was assigned to the abbey at Sacromonte and also as a professor of canon law at the University of Granada. He passed the gypsy quarter every day on his way back and forth between the abbey and the university, and he saw that something had to be done for the gypsy youngsters and other poor children of the quarter who were left on their own by their families and society in general. He eventually established six schools in Granada, which he linked into a group called "Escuelas del Ave Maria" and which are administered by a directorate of leading citizens of the city. They cover kindergarten through high school, and also vocational training. Their total enrollment is now 4,000. The original school on Sacromonte has 360 students, from 6 to 14 years of age, in the boys' branch and 320 in the girls', and many of them are from gypsy families. The Sacro-monte school is free, and the state pays the salaries of teachers. In the other Ave Maria schools a moderate tuition is charged. The training methods at the other schools in the group follow orthodox patterns generally; the Sacromonte school continues to accent the learn-by-playing technique, and new visual methods are now being developed. All teachers are civilians, and the general director may also be one. The present general director of the Ave Maria group is a young priest from the Granada coast village of Motril, Father José Montero, who studied pedagogy at Louvain for four years before being ordained in 1956.

Don Andrés was near 80 when he died in 1923. He is buried in a chapel at the side of the schoolyard. There is no monument of any kind, no marker—not the slightest sign of where he is buried. He had left instructions saying he wished no memorial. His only request was to be buried on the school grounds.

The Alhambra

On January 2, 1492, Queen Isabella unfurled the colors of the king-dom of Castile on the Tower of La Vela (Watchtower) of the Alham-bra. That was the day the Moorish empire in Spain officially came to an end. As Boabdil, the last king of the Moors, made his way into exile on the Alpujarra slopes of the Sierra Nevada, he looked for the last time at the kingdom he had lost. Tradition has named the summit from which he looked as "The Hill of Tears." In his *Tales of the Alhambra* Washington Irving relates that Boabdil's mother added to his misery by upbraiding him. "You do well," said she, "to weep as a woman over what you could not defend as a man."

When this episode was later told to Charles I, Washington Irving says, the crusty king remarked: "Had I been he or he been I, I would rather have made this Alhambra my sepulchre, than have lived with-out a kingdom in the Alpujarra."

Mighty words indeed! But Washington Irving observes: "How easy it is for those in power and prosperity to preach heroism to the vanquished! How little can they understand that life itself may rise in value with the unfortunate, when nought but life remains."

It was not easy for Washington Irving himself to abandon Granada. He took his last look at the city late in the day and then hurried to be out of sight of the Alhambra before sunset. He wanted to carry away a recollection of it "clothed in all its beauty," he explained.

Perhaps a similar thought is in the minds of many of the visitors who nowadays attend the International Music and Ballet festival each summer in the Alhambra palaces and in the open-air theater in the Generalifé gardens. For those unmoved by Granada the late Mexican poet, Francisco de Icaza, who lived in Granada for many years early in this century, had something to say. His words are engraved in stone at the entrance to the gardens at the foot of the Tower of La Vela. He says:

> Give him alms, good woman,
> As in one's life there isn't
> A misfortune so great
> As being blind to Granada.

Castile

Spain means castles—particularly those in Castile. Castles and Castile are linked as closely as the bull and the matador. The Latin word *castellum* (or *castrum*) for "fortress" became *castillo* in Spanish. So many castles were erected in the historic and geographical center of Spain that the region naturally acquired the name Castilla or, as we say in English, Castile.

The boom in castle-building got under way early in the eighth century, shortly after the Christian Reconquest of Spain was started. Lines of fortresses were methodically strung across Spain. Each time a piece of land was won back from the Moors, a new front was staked out with a castle as the snug keystone. The castles help preserve the lean beauty, the mystic aura, and the austere splendor of Castile.

Castile is literally the heart of Spain, stretching down the center of the country from the chill waters of the Bay of Biscay on the north to the sunny outlines of Andalusia, 500 miles to the south. It occupies more than a third of the entire area of Spain. As if it were a precious jewel set upon a table in the middle of a room for everyone to gaze at and admire, Castile rests on a high plateau, called a *meseta*. Spaniards from other parts of the country teasingly say that half the landscape in Castile is the sky. But what a sky! Velasquez did his best to show the luminosity and the sharp brilliance of Castile's skies, but some people say that they are even more enchanting than he made them out to be.

The northern part of Castile is described as Castilla la Vieja, Old Castile; the southern, Castilla la Nueva, New Castile. The Old Castile area was liberated from the Moors first. It was only in the latter cen-

Madrid balances the modern look of high-rise buildings with bright flower boxes on the pedestrian-restraining wall near the city's main plaza

93

turies of the campaign of reconquest that the Spaniards won back the southern part of Castile—and that is the reason for the adjective *new* even though the winning-back took place a long time ago. Famous names are among the provinces of both Old and New Castile. Santander, Burgos, Logroño, Segovia, Soria, Avila, Valladolid, and Palencia are the provinces of Old Castile. New Castile is composed of the provinces of Madrid, Toledo, Ciudad Real, Cuenca, and Guadalajara. Each provincial capital has the same name as the province itself. Let's look first at Old Castile.

Spain's renowned Escorial, the palace-church-and-royal burial place built by Philip II on the plains of Castile not far from Madrid

The Alcazar, a former fortress at Segovia, is now a popular museum

Old Castile

Our look has to be literally upward because the *meseta* holding Old Castile averages 2,300 feet above sea level. Mountain ranges rumple the perimeter of the *meseta*, except for the western side which slants toward Portugal. The mountains discourage the winds that bring moisture from the sea, with the result that most of the rain is dumped on the slopes bordering the *meseta* and little is carried into the interior. Winters are long and summers are searing. A favorite saying of people of Old Castile is that they have nine months of winter and three months of hell's fire. Just about all brooks and streams empty into the Douro, making it by far the principal river of the region. It travels nearly 500 miles in Castile and western Spain before entering Portugal. The Ebro River rises in the northeast corner of the region near the border with the Basque country, but heads for the Mediterranean.

One of the most spectacular tributaries of the Ebro is the Jalón which originates among the empty, stark stones of the Sierra Ministra in Soria province. The name Jalón has a Moorish ring and, indeed, this area had a big role in the struggle of Spaniards to reconquer their homeland. The most renowned of the Arab generals, Almanzor, died in the city of Medinaceli in the Jalón district after having been defeated on the neighboring fields. This historic district is impressively robust. "We are in the highest district in Spain," Ortega y Gasset wrote. "We are walking on the shoulders of a giant."

Old Castile's economy is based on agriculture, wheat being the chief product. The region is known as "the Breadbasket of Spain." Santander, along the sea at the northern end of Old Castile, is Spain's principal dairy province. Sheepraising is particularly extensive in the provinces of Palencia, Soria, and Burgos. Wines from Old Castile rank with the best and vineyards flank the banks of the Douro. Logroño province is said to produce the best table wines in the country. But industry is gradually taking hold in the region. The shipyards at Santander build and repair vessels of ocean-going size. A major automobile assembly plant has been established in Valladolid province, and the northern part of Old Castile is rich in coal and iron deposits which are helping to spur industrial development. New industry is also being generated by the panoply of rivers which make available an important supply of hydroelectric power.

Most of all, Old Castile is renowned as Spain's leading source of history. Each province has been the setting for more than one pivotal event in the development of the Spanish nation. Santander is riddled with ancient caves whose walls are filled with paintings that tell us about the people who lived in the area before the recording of history began. The Castilian language, considered to be the most perfect form of Spanish, originated in Old Castile, and Logroño province was the

96

birthplace of Gonzalo de Berceo, the first poet known to have written in Castilian. El Cid, the warrior hero of the greatest epic in the Castilian language, raced across the peninsula from Burgos city to do battle with the Moors. During the Spanish Civil War the nationalist forces first used Salamanca as their base, but General Franco soon shifted the headquarters to Burgos city and from here fought on to final victory. Near the capital of Soria province are the ruins of the old Celt-Iberian city of Numancia where the inhabitants fought the Roman invaders for a score of years and then, when convinced everything was in vain, took their own lives to avoid capture by the legionaires of Scipio. Painters and poets have broadcast the beauties of Segovia, especially its aqueduct and cathedral. The capital of Palencia province has the distinction of being the birthplace of Spain's first university early in the thirteenth century. After the experiment was proved successful, the trail-blazing university was moved outside of Castile to Salamanca.

A statue of St. Teresa dominates the square named in her honor in Avila, the Castilian town where she was born

The great holy woman and spiritual writer, the mystic Saint Teresa, was born in the capital of Avila, a melancholy city of donkey carts and a huge medieval wall. Spaniards and others remember her advice:

> Let nothing disturb thee,
> Let nothing affright thee;
> All things are passing,
> God never changeth.
> Patient endurance
> Attaineth to all things.
> Who has God,
> In nothing is wanting.

New Castile

The plateau of New Castile is not as high as that of Old Castile, averaging not more than 2,000 feet in altitude. What makes the climate pleasant is that winters do not last long while summers fade away slowly. The main rivers are the Tagus and the Guadiana, and Spain shares both of these—like the Douro—with Portugal. The Tagus is the longest river on the peninsula. It is 625 miles long and more than 550 miles of this is in Spain. Rain in New Castile is less frequent than in the north, but an extensive irrigation network is bringing new lands into cultivation all the time. Sage, thyme, and rosemary flourish on the hills of Guadalajara province, and much honey is produced. Along with wheat, the lands of New Castile supply olives and fine wines in abundance. Such hot-weather crops as cotton and tobacco are also grown. Farming and cattle-raising are the main occupations of New Castile, but industry is expanding. The most important hydroelectric ensemble on the Continent has been built in the mountains of Guadalajara province, and at Zorita in the same province in July, 1968, Spain's first nuclear reactor to produce electricity was inaugurated. It is the first of a series which in ten years will reach an annual output of 40,000 million kilowatt hours. Ciudad Real (and the somewhat larger La Mancha zone) lacks trees, but instead has splendid windmills including the one with which Don Quixote tilted. For La Mancha is where Don Quixote was "born," and where this fascinating human being searched for his Lady Dulcinea.

The city of Toledo, the seat of the Church in Spain since the first days of Christianity, has been declared a national monument by the government. Until the religious persecutions of the fifteenth century, Jew, Moslem, and Christian lived and prospered side by side, and together contributed to the cultural prosperity of their city. The Synagogue of El Transito was built in the fourteenth century in Mudéjar style—an architectural form which ingeniously blended the delicate, ornate brickwork of the Moors with the sturdy Romanesque workmanship of the Christians, and brought East and West together. Domenikos Theotokopoulos, the artist from Crete who became known as El Greco, embellished churches and other holy places in Toledo with paintings that rank with the finest ever created.

Madrid

Philip II wished to establish his capital at the center of his kingdom and in 1561 moved the royal court from Toledo to Madrid. The Hill of the Angels, which is considered to be the geographical center of the Iberian peninsula, is but a half dozen miles from Madrid. When Philip II died, his successor, Philip III, decided in 1601 to transfer the capital to Valladolid. That lasted only a short time and in 1606 Madrid definitely became the capital. At the time of being chosen the capital of the world's largest monarchy, Madrid was an agricultural center with not more than 25,000 residents. Great changes have taken place since then. In 1935 the population reached the million mark, and 24 years later a new-born baby girl became the 2-millionth inhabitant of Madrid. With the exception of Tokyo, Madrid is said to be the fastest-growing capital in the world—city authorities know that in 1969 Madrid's population will reach 3 million. Madrid is sprawled across an ever-wider section of the New Castile *meseta* at a height of 2,200 feet. It is the highest capital in Europe. It is also one of the busiest. Madrid has shed the somber, staid appearance of a classic city of Castile, and is alive and full of energy. More than half of Madrid jobs are in the government, in banks and business offices, in shops, in the ateliers of artisans, and in such service industries as travel agencies, hotels, and cafés. Madrid has long been a commercial center but the

The formal gardens of the royal palace in Madrid, the highest capital in Europe

city's growing industrialization became noticeable just before the start of World War II. Now almost 40 per cent of the people work in factories. There are 12,000 plants in the metropolitan area making everything from washing machines to automobiles. The industrial development is taking place *around* rather than *within* Madrid, and this has encouraged residents to say that the city has a Red Belt like the one in Paris. Officials believe that the description is more picturesque than realistic, and that today's higher standard of living has taken the sharpness and significance from the term.

The work week in Madrid is still six days, with even banks open on Saturdays, although during the summer many neighborhood stores close on Saturday afternoons. Government offices keep banking hours—that is, 9 a.m. to 2 p.m. daily except Sunday. Most shops close at lunchtime from 1 p.m. to 4 p.m., and in the summer to 4:30 p.m. or 5 p.m.

100

Throughout the year daily closing time is 8 p.m. at the latest, except for tobacco shops which remain open until 9 p.m. Street-corner vendors with small "stands" consisting of a wooden tray set upon a folding chair sell cigarettes "after hours," and so do some cafés. The sidewalk vendors work out prices with the customers but the cafés post a sign declaring that they are authorized by the government to charge 5 per cent more than the usual price.

Every downtown corner has at least one man or woman selling lottery tickets. Prices of these tickets vary because at certain times of the year there are special high-stakes prizes. But any day in the week one can buy a ticket for as little as 2 pesetas and stand to win as much as 2,500 pesetas in the daily lottery. Blind men are often the lottery ticket-sellers. Many people, both for humane reasons and "for luck,"

A vendor in Madrid's flea market, the Raatro, tries to get the attention of some customers

*Lotteries are popular
throughout the Iberian
peninsula. In a suburb of
Oporto, lottery-ticket sellers
adopt a unique form of
advertising*

will buy their tickets from the same blind man regularly. Often they will ask him to pick out the ticket for them. Football is extremely popular in Madrid and the city's team, Real Madrid, has been the European champion a number of times in recent years. Weekend football games provide an opportunity for Madrileños to guess the winners and win big cash prizes. About a fourth of the money bet in these "football pools" is used for the general development of sports throughout the country, and it is not an inconsiderable sum. In a recent year more than 500 million pesetas was spent in this way.

Public Transportation

The people of Madrid depend on public transportation to travel between their home and their job, and for shopping and other trips around the city. Subway lines are stretching out to the new communities which are sprouting like esparto grass on the fringes of Madrid. The Madrid subway fare of 2 pesetas is one of the lowest in the world. The subway cars are large, are painted white on the inside, and do not have many seats. They also do not carry any advertising cards. In Barcelona, subway stations are given numbers as well as names, which simplifies travel for foreigners and people who can read numbers but not words. The Madrid subway uses only names. In general, the Madrid subway is modern but in one way it has not kept up with the times. The fine for smoking or carrying a lighted cigar is 5 pesetas. At today's prices, the cheapest cigar costs more than that.

Taxi rates are low, compared to what they are in other world capitals. The minimum fare is 10 pesetas and the average ride costs less than 25. Nonetheless, taxis are beyond the reach of the average Madrid resident as a daily habit. The bus company has introduced a "microbus" which is something of a compromise between taxis and the regular busses. A microbus carries only 20 passengers (less than half the capacity of a regular bus) and each passenger is assured a seat. When all the seats are filled the driver puts a *completo* sign in the windshield. Another advantage of the microbus is that it will stop almost anywhere along its route to let passengers off. Smoking is also permitted. And for all this a microbus charges only one peseta more than the regular bus fare of 4 pesetas.

Saber Vivir

Madrid people are noted for their *saber vivir*—their knowledge of how to live—and the prosperity of recent years has enabled them to spend larger sums of money on their wardrobe. Men are just as careful as women in the way they dress, and a man may be as fussy as any woman in choosing a pair of shoes. The average man prefers a shoe with a pointed toe and a thin sole to the heavy British-oxford type. Solid traditional colors are preferred for suits, and most men (like the women) have their clothes custom-made. Ready-to-wear articles are making some headway but slowly. In recent months boutiques with young people's fashions have been established in the general area of the Calle Don Ramon de la Cruz, which is named after an eighteenth-century writer. *Moncho* is a diminutive form for "Ramon" and young Spaniards, with their orientation toward American ways and habits, refer to Calle Don Ramon de la Cruz as "Moncho Street."

Around 7 o'clock each evening teen-agers gather in the *Drugstore, Bourbon Street,* and other modernistically furnished café-bars in the Moncho Street neighborhood, playing juke-boxes, conferring on school assignments, or just talking. Their favorite drink is Coca-Cola, although some of the boys often drink beer and the girls might have a small glass of wine. Spanish bars are stocked with alcoholic beverages as strong as any in the world but they also serve a wide line of soft drinks. Many bars specializing in alcoholic drinks also have an espresso machine, and many coffee-bars also have some wines, beers, and high-alcoholic-content beverages available. An adult in a Madrid bar is as likely to ask for a small bottle of mineral water as a glass of brandy and, whether the order is for liquor or a soft drink, the waiter or bartender serving it might be a 14-year-old boy. There is no general law prohibiting young people from frequenting places where liquor is served. But an adult in Spain would never give a young person anything but wine or beer, and a Spanish youth would never think of ordering whisky or any other highly alcoholic drink in a café or bar.

Another interesting characteristic of the Spanish way of life is that teen-agers never forget what time it is during the evening. Well before 10 p.m. the groups of young people in a Madrid café will begin thinning out. By 10 p.m. all the teen-agers will have left. Ten o'clock is the traditional going-home hour not only for the young but for adults. In the early evening hours, people on the way home from work, university students, married couples—Madrileños in general—crowd neighborhood and downtown bars to have an *aperitivo*—usually, a small glass of wine that can cost as little as 2 pesetas. In some bars, as in the Calle de Echegaray, *aperitivo* time is enlivened by men singers and musicians who sing songs of Andalusia and keep time by slapping the four fingers of one hand against the heel of the other in a staccato crescendo that becomes so excruciatingly sharp and intense it makes some listeners close their eyes. But at 10 p.m. the *aperitivo* hour ends, and the people head for home or a restaurant.

There are also late-evening movies, plays, and musical performances, but these are for only a small percentage of the population. Going to the movies is almost as formal as attending the theater or an opera because tickets must be bought in advance for one of the day's several performances. A couple interested in the late-evening show will buy the tickets before dinner or before *aperitivo* time—reserving their seats. In summer, during fiestas, on Saturdays, and on the eves of holidays, the evening is extended somewhat. But, in general, Madrid goes home early and young people, unless accompanied by adults, are off the streets long before midnight. There are, of course, elegant bars with dim lights, recorded music, and divans in the general area of the Castellana Hilton Hotel, and they remain open as long as there are customers. A half-pint bottle of tonic water in these places costs at least 50 pesetas, wine is not served (except for champagne) and the language of the clientele is likely to be English or French.

The "Hanging Houses" add a spectacular touch to the scenery of Cuenca in New Castile

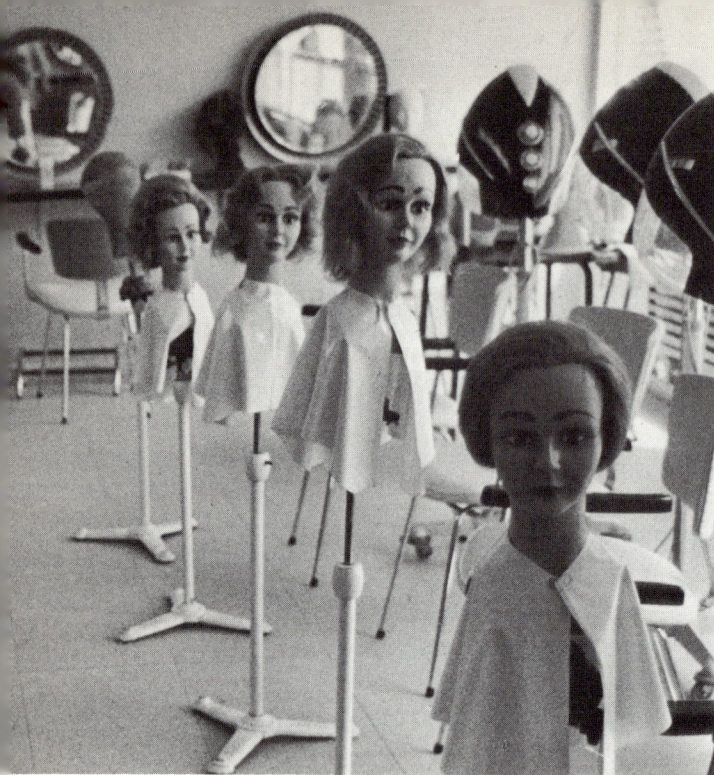

A classroom where hair-dressing is taught at Senara, an Opus Dei school for girls in Madrid

Educational System

Despite the increasing number of state-operated public schools, most of the elementary and secondary schools are private or are operated by religious groups. School starts at the age of six and for youngsters not going on to the *liceo*, Secondary School, ends at 14 (the minimum legal age at which children may leave school). Those who plan to continue studying after they have become 14 transfer from the regular Primary School at the age of ten to the Secondary School, where they study for their *bachillerato* which certifies that a student has completed his secondary studies. The Secondary School is divided into two sections—students aged from 10 to 14, and those from 14 through 16. The first is called the elementary section; the other, the senior. The student wishing to attend a university after getting his *bachillerato* must first do preparatory studies for a year. The course of study for the 10-to-14-year-olds in the elementary section of Secondary School is somewhat more difficult than that of the same age group in the

106

Primary School. The *baohillerato* candidates, for instance, have Latin along with a modern language (which are not taught in Primary School), and the other subjects, such as Mathematics and Spanish Literature, are a bit more advanced. There is now a tendency to make both courses the same and even to give both of them in the Primary School.

Students interested in technical training remain in the Primary School till they are 12 years old and then go to a vocational center where, on reaching 17 after a five-year course, they can qualify as an apprentice in one of many trades and specialties. If they remain for two additional years at the vocational center they can be certified as a master in their specialty.

Primary Schools and the vocational training centers are free, but in the Secondary Schools (and universities) a small *matricula*, "registration fee," is charged. This fee amounts to about 350 pesetas a term for each subject. The *matricula* is reduced for parents of large families, and those parents with eight, or more, children do not pay a *matricula* for any of them as long as the oldest child going to school is not over 23. Part of the *matricula* is returned if a student gets a perfect mark in a subject (10 is the highest possible mark; 5 is Sufficient, or Passing; anything below 5 is Insufficient, and the subject has to be retaken. (There are cases where students repeat a particular subject two or three times). Scholarships, both for Secondary Schools and universities, are made available by the government and private institutions for students who are from poor families and/or are of above-average intelligence.

Students work hard, attending class six days a week. The average Primary and Secondary-School schedule is 9 a.m. to 1:30 p.m. and 3:30 p.m. to 6:30 p.m. but there are no afternoon classes on Wednesdays and Saturdays. (University schedules vary with the course.) Religion is in the curriculum, but non-Catholic parents can request that their children be excused from that class.

There are few problems of discipline in Spain's schools. Even in state schools a child can be expelled for disciplinary reasons. Boys, of course, are the ones who usually cause any trouble there is. At the beginning of the term each student starts off with a perfect score of 10 in Deportment. Boys being boys, they lose points as the term progresses—and some faster than others. If a student's grade drops to 0, his parents are called in for a conference and, after appropriate promises all around, he starts again with a perfect score of 10. If he loses these ten points he is expelled. A woman teacher in a state Secondary School for boys notes that there is no talking back to teacher, either. "The boys are on their feet when I enter the classroom," she says, "and they do not sit down till I sit down."

Building For The Future

So much building is going on in the Madrid area that a large percentage of the city's workers are employed in the construction industry. Even the fringes of Madrid, ignored for a long time, are becoming more livable. One of the once-overlooked areas is Pozo di Tio Raimundo ("Uncle Raymond's Well") which used to be a festering shanty-town where even children could not walk in the streets after a rain because the dirt roads had turned into mud. The Pozo di Tio Raimundo, a half dozen miles from the Puerta del Sol, still does not look like an ideal retirement area, but for the 80,000 residents it is the best place they have ever lived. It has been built up by the people themselves with the help of a unique team of university students and a Jesuit priest, Father José-Maria Llanos, S.J., now in his sixties. While a chaplain at Madrid university, the Jesuit and four undergraduates decided to move in with the squatters at Pozo di Tio Raimundo in the fall of 1955. They had no evangelization program in mind. Their basic idea was to live among the people and continue their own regular work and studies in Madrid.

In those days most of the people in Pozo di Tio Raimundo had just arrived from Andalusia, hoping for jobs. It was idle agricultural land, not zoned for housing. A typical family rented or bought a small piece of land cheaply and, with all the members of the family and with friends pitching in, built a room with a roof over it. They worked fast (usually at night) to get the roof on because with a roof the structure became a domicile, and was no longer a shanty that could be knocked

108

A typical house in a shanty-town of Madrid. Once numerous, these shanty-towns are gradually being eliminated, and residents are moving to low-cost housing units

down by the police. Father Llanos and the four university students built a three-room house for themselves. Soon people began dropping by with their problems. The team decided it was not right for them to live in the area, going to work in Madrid every day, and leaving their neighbors to work out their own problems. They began night classes for the adults. There was no electricity in the area, and the only available water was brought in on little carts and sold at relatively high prices by enterprising merchants from the city. The team organized cooperatives among the people for water, for electricity, and for construction. Almost a year after the team had arrived in the area, a high government housing official paid a visit and was astounded at all the building activity—none of it legal! "It was like an Arab village in full movement," Fernando Helena, one of the university students on the team recalls.

"We are Spaniards—we have a right to have a house," was the attitude of the squatters. The official outlined a general building plan and the manner for getting the housing program into legal channels. Within a month the legalized program, backed by government money, was in operation. For the next two years, the government official came every Sunday to observe the progress. And progress is still being made. The original team is intact except for one of the four former students; the three remaining students have married and have families, and are part of the community. The Jesuit and his team continue to operate a night school for working young men and women, and have built a vocational training school for 600 boys and girls. At assembly each morning the youngsters pray for all children in the world, and a flag of some country is raised. It is a different flag each day, every country having its turn. There are no exceptions—Communist bloc or West; black, yellow, or white; regardless of its religion or absence of religion. The purpose of the Jesuit is to teach the youngsters of Pozo di Tio Raimundo that all boys and girls in the world are children of God.

Progress and Tradition

Because it is the capital of Spain Madrid gets special attention. Its mayor *(alcade)* is named by the head of state for a six-year term. The Alcade of Barcelona and the mayors of provincial capitals are nominated by the Minister of the Interior *(Gobernación)* for 12 years. The civil governors of provinces name the mayors of other towns. The 36 members of the Madrid city council, like the *concejales* ("councilmen") in other cities, are elected by popular vote. On becoming the Alcade of Madrid in 1965, Don Carlos Arias Navarro launched a newsworthy series of "operations." The first was Operation Asphalt in

110

which workmen, laboring at night in the summer of 1966, repaved 120 miles of Madrid streets. That was followed at Christmas by Operation Alumbrado which put brighter, American-style mercury lamps atop 45,000 tall standards along 500 miles of streets. To ease the traffic situation, underground parking garages and overpasses and under-passes at critical congestion points were started. The overpass at the Atocha railway terminal was the first of the traffic projects to be com-pleted, and Madrileños quickly christened it *Scalextric,* the name for a children's toy, because it appeared to be assembled so easily.

Young boys and girls are invited each year by city authorities to use brush or pencil, colors or ink, to tell how the city looks to them. Several hundred youngsters respond to the invitation and the setting of the com-petition might be a temporarily idle runway at Barazas airport, the Prado gardens, or the Plaza de la Armeria outside the royal palace. Prizes are brushes, easels, and other drawing materials. A few years ago an American teen-age boy, whose father was stationed at the U.S. military base on the outskirts of Madrid, submitted a painting of a main gateway of the Retiro park, and his painting was used as the front and back cover of the city's cultural magazine, *Villa de Madrid.*

The best-known family of young people in Madrid are the grand-children of General Franco—one boy and seven girls. Their father, Dr. Cristobal Martinez Bordiú, is a heart surgeon. He also has the title of Marqués de Villaverde and his wife (General Franco's daughter) is usually referred to as the Marquesa de Villaverde rather than Carmen Franco (her maiden name). All the girls in the family have names beginning with Maria. The oldest, 17-year-old Maria del Carmen has the same name as her mother, Carmen being a favorite name through-out Spain because the Virgin of Carmel is a protector of navigators. The other girls are named Maria del Mar (or Mariola, "for Hope"), Maria de la O (a Virgin honored in Seville), Maria Aránzazu (a Basque Virgin), and so on. Their 15-year-old brother has the same first—as well as *family*—name as his grandfather, Francisco Franco, instead of the family name of his father. In Spain it is traditional for the father's family name to be handed down from one generation to another. Since General Franco and his wife, Doña Carmen Polo de Franco, had only

Two volunteers solicit donations on National Charity Day in Madrid

one child—and this child was a daughter—there was no possibility of continuing his family name. A happy solution was found when the Minister of Justice issued a decree formally authorizing the baby son of General Franco's daughter to be baptized as Francisco Franco.

Throughout the year in Madrid there are several public collection drives—Charity Day, Red Cross, Cancer, the Missions, and the like. Teen-age school girls, working in pairs, do the street-corner collecting, pinning badges on the contributors with a system of colors matching the size of the gift. Wives of ministers, princesses, and other women of social standing also assist in the drives. They are assigned to outdoor booths at the entrances to ministries, the City Hall, and other prominent buildings. "Booths" is not quite the word, perhaps, because the canopy covering the working site of the society women is almost as striking as a Bernini baldachin. The canopies are made with heavy crimson velour drapes, and fitted out with Persian rugs and gilded chairs and tables. The ladies let their friends know in advance at which booth they will be on duty, and it behooves anyone wishing to avoid becoming *persona non grata* in social circles to appear punctiliously, and to make a noteworthy gift for the sake of charity. While booth-tenders, such as Princess Sofia (the wife of Don Juan Carlos) and Dutch Princess Irene (the wife of the Carlist pretender to the throne) wait for their friends to arrive bearing gifts, music is provided by a martial band.

Madrileños like a fiesta, and in Madrid (as throughout Castile) the cause of merriment is often built around a patron saint or a holy day. Yet, no matter how solemn the religious ceremony or occasion the fiesta is capped by a bullfight. San Isidore the Farmer is Madrid's patron. He was born near Madrid in 1070. When he took time off in the fields to pray, Madrid people say, the angels would appear and push the plow for him so that he could get his farm work done. There are special bull-fights when Madrid celebrates his feast in May, and excitement is added by permitting the people to inspect the herd of bulls from which are chosen the ones to be fought in the fiesta's *corridas*. Sunday is the traditional spring-to-fall bullfight day in Madrid but during the week-long San Isidore fiesta there are *corridas* every day.

On St. Anthony's feast, young girls (particularly seamstresses) make the traditional visit to the church named for him near the Segovia bridge, and beseech his help in finding a fiancé. They cover their heads with white mantillas, and over their shoulders they wear silk *mantóns de Manila,* named after Manila, a Madrid seamstress of some generations ago. (The *mantón*, a triangular scarf embroidered with a flower design, was exclusively a covering for a piano until Manila wrapped one around her shoulders to go to St. Anthony's feast one year.) At St. Anthony's church the young girls drop a pin in the holy-water font, saying: *Al Santo, como siempre*—"To the saint, as always."

For all its size, sophistication, and cosmopolitan manner, Madrid is a traditional Castilian city at heart.

113

The Basque Country

Lope de Vega said that the Basque country is a paradise and extremely delightful to look upon. The Basque people know that he was not exaggerating, or being poetically polite. The Basques believe that when the earth was being settled they were assigned a special part of it on which to make their homes. They were not given a large area, but no one complains about that. The Basque country is composed of three provinces (Álava, Vizcaya, and Guipúzcoa), and they are among the nation's smallest. They are bunched into 2,750 square miles in that northern part of Spain which shares the Bay of Biscay with the southwestern corner of France. A fourth province, Navarre, is sometimes included in the Basque country because many of its valleys are inhabited by Basques.

Three Basque *départements,* or provinces, are on the French side of the border, along the slopes of the Pyrenees. The Spanish Basques do not have the Pyrenees in their frontyard the way their French brothers do, but they are not short of mountains by any means. The Spanish coastline is paralleled a short distance inland by the Cantabrian Mountains and some *peñas* ("peaks") are almost a mile high. When the peculiar warm south wind, which Pierre Loti wrote about, blows, the air becomes so clear that mountains which were the backdrop for the setting suddenly appear at center stage, sharply outlined. The ill part of this wind is that after all the dreamy balminess, the clouds may group together for a terrible thunderstorm. Rains, as well as fog and mist, are frequent, and it is decidedly a wet climate. September and January are the months when there are exceptionally heavy seas, and

A scull prepares to pass under the bridge at San Sebastián in the Basque Country

115

the waters leap up on the shore, washing away, or at least damaging, everything in their path. Sometimes this spectacular of high wild tides lasts a week.

Trees are one of the traditional riches of the Basques, and since earliest times have been carefully protected. In olden days the wood chopper followed a set ritual, asking forgiveness of the tree that he was going to chop down, and anyone who felled a tree had to replace it with two new ones.

Corn, potatoes, and fine beef-cattle are grown but industry and mining form the base of the Basque economy and are the main source of wealth. Steel and paper manufacturing are the major industries. Although not given the best land or climate, the Basques have made the most out of what is theirs. The Basque country is wealthy, and to see that for yourself all you have to do is look around. It is obviously a region that is well developed and where everyone works. What is particularly noteworthy is that the Basques *like* to work.

Origin and Language of the Basques

Everything is known about the Basques except one elemental vital fact: What is their origin? No one knows where they come from, and this mystery about their origin, as well as the unique language they speak, makes the Basques especially interesting. Some who have studied the Basque people say that they might be the oldest race in the world, but no one has been able to pinpoint their beginnings. Theories are many. One is that they originally emigrated from the Caucasus or even further east. A general theory is that they are the descendants of the Iberians who, after the many invasions of the peninsula by peoples from the north, south, and east, were finally pushed into a mean corner by the Pyrenees—and survived! The mountains not only protected and conserved them, but also isolated them from the rest of the world. The Basque country was the last part of Spain to be Romanized, and also the last to be Christianized. As late as the ninth century, the Basques followed a naturalist religion in which their gods were the wonders of nature. Thunder and lightning were deities which they respected. The sun had great importance for them, and they gave it such titles as "The

116

Basques love to bet, but better luck next time: Pamplona residents are unsuccessful in their bids to win the household appliances on display

Eye of Light" and even "The Eye of God." On the facades of old buildings and gravestones the sun is frequently represented.

The real miracle is that after so long a passage of time and so many generations, the Basques have survived as an identifiable race. Two million people now live in the Basque country (including Navarre) and about half of them are Basques. (The population in the French Basque *départements* is nearly the same.) The Basques have distinctive racial characteristics—physically they are short and stocky, but strong. Struggles to turn a ragged land into a paradise—and the constant battle for survival—helped form them physically and temperamentally. All the old-fashioned virtues, such as honesty, loyalty, and industriousness, are theirs. They make a cult of keeping their word. They are not much for talking, and if the person they are with wishes to remain silent, they will not chatter idly. In a poem about the Basques, Tirso de Molina said they are small in words but big in deeds. Everywhere they go, from the Americas to Australia, it is recognized that the Basques are hard workers with plenty of initiative.

Basques like to eat, and eat better and with more variety than other Spaniards. Food is such a passion with them that there are numerous gastronomic societies, which are open only to men. But this is not the passive type of food appreciation in which chefs prepare the meals and amateur gourmets sample them. In the gastronomic societies of the Basque country the men do both the cooking and the feasting.

The Basques are extremely proud of being Basques even if—or, perhaps, because—it makes them different from their fellow Spaniards. They have a great pride in everything that is theirs—from the land in which they live to the language they speak among themselves. Language detectives have not been able to track down the beginnings of the Basque language. Its origin is as mysterious as the people who speak it. Here again there are theories, and they range from the language of the Caucasus to that of Pakistan. Many believe that the Basque language is the very language that the Iberians spoke. In any case it is completely different from what other people on the Iberian peninsula speak today. In Spanish, for instance, the way to say Basque country is *El Pais Vasco;* in the Basque language, one says *Euskalerria.* The Spanish word for the Basque language is *Vascuence,* while the Basques call it *Euskera.*

Mysteriously, certain Basque words have their echoes in distant places. One fascinating example of how human speech traveled across the world long before the days of the printing press is the Basque word for water, *Ur.* Almost anywhere one looks on a map of the world—from Abraham's Valley of the Ur to Lake Uri in Japan to the Ural Mountains and Ural River in Russia—the old Basque word shows up in the name of a body of water or of a place associated with water. In the United States, for instance, we have Lake Huron.

Even before the Romans arrived in France and on the Iberian peninsula the people spoke Basque, and in recent generations it was spoken in a wide area of northern Spain. Today Basque children speak Spanish in school, and the only chance to develop—or even to learn—Basque is in the home.

Race and language have been not only the primary source of pride for the Basque people but also the sole symbols of their unity. In the development of the Spanish nation they have never been politically independent, and as the Reconquest seesawed over the centuries the Basques alternately were part of the kingdom of Castile or of Navarre.

In the nineteenth century the Liberalism spirit of France (and the rest of Europe) swept into Spain, and when it appeared that their nation was going to ride with the tide not all the Basques were happy. Some Basques decided to have nothing more to do with Spain, and began to think of separatism. The urging of autonomy for the Basque people became a political movement in 1931 when the Second Republic succeeded the monarchy. The provisional government promised the Basques autonomy and, right in the middle of the Civil War, gave it to them. However, the autonomy lasted only until the end of the war. The desire for a greater say in their affairs has not disappeared, although it seems that the vast majority of modern-day Basques are proud regionalists rather than separatists. But traces of separatism still remain. In mid-summer of 1968 the secret-police chief of Guipúzcoa province was shot to death at his apartment door when he was returning home at midday, and his murder was attributed to a terrorist group of Basque nationalists. Some weeks earlier, in June, a traffic policeman was shot by two terrorists when he stopped their car. The killings of the policemen came after several months of growing violence by Basque nationalists. In an effort to track down the murderers, and to put an end to the violence, the Spanish government took the unusual step of suspending the constitutional provisions against unauthorized searches and seizures of persons and property by police in Guipúzcoa province. In the decree suspending civil rights the government said a climate of violence had been created by "agitators who follow the instigations of clandestine groups, supported from abroad."

Sports, Dances, and Songs

The Basques have been described as a people who jump and dance atop the Pyrenees. All Basque sports are games requiring great physical strength and, with the exception of *pelota* (jai alai), originated in day-to-day work—chopping tree trunks, lifting heavy stones, mowing a field, and so forth. All of these daily tasks became competitive sports

119

A family makes mealtime a picnic on a train ride through the Basque Country

performed before enthusiastic spectators. After the Basques decide who is the strongest man in this or that category, or who can do some job the fastest, they let their animals compete. For example, whose ox can drag a block of granite through the village in the shortest time? Such sports not only generate great emotion among the onlookers but also a great deal of betting. The Basques love to bet, and will bet on anything. Fights between goats used to be a boisterous target of betters, but all contests between animals have been prohibited by law. (They are still organized clandestinely, however.)

120

Pelota, the only sport not connected with the way Basques used to earn a living, is also the only one that is not really Basque. But the Basques are such masters of it that their name is automatically linked with it. On a *frontón* as big as a football field they scoop up the ball with a huge wicker bat shaped like a question-mark and, unquestionably, fire it back at speeds of up to two miles a minute.

Their dances, too, are virile and lively; among the several dozen, perhaps the main one is the *aurresku*. It is the dance that highlights every festive occasion, and when officials or important guests are present they are invited to lead the dancing. The *aurresku*, although an ancient dance, is nowhere near as simple as an old-time foxtrot or as graceful as a turn-of-the-century Viennese waltz. It is more like a routine that has been choreographed for a professional group of dancers. Its theme is actively militant, and the dancers step, two-step, and about-face through the whole classic gamut of war, starting with the stirring call to arms and ending, breathless and jubilant, at the inevitable and well-merited victory.

Song comes easy to the Basques. When you have three Basques together, it is said, you have a chorus. The Basques sing best when singing in their language. Their songs usually are about the sea, the fields, animals, and religious subjects. What they sing depends on their mood and the occasion. On an outing, when everyone is feeling happy, they might sing a rousing sailor's song, *Boga Boga;* after all, the Basques are seafaring people. "Row, row, sailor," the song urges merrily. "We have to travel very far, very far; as far as the Indies." The Basques like to remind themselves, and everyone else, that the round-the-world voyage begun by Magellan was completed by a Basque, and young people pronounce his name, Juan Sebastian Elcano, as evenly and formally as the name Franklin Delano Roosevelt is pronounced in the United States.

Another popular song is addressed to a little bird. "Where are you going, white dove?" the song asks. "All the mountains of Spain are covered with snow. Come spend the night in my house." Young people today are as likely, when they are in the mood, to sing an American Negro spiritual as a traditional Basque religious song such as *Agur Javnak* ("Good-bye, my Lord").

Maite is a Basque folk song that appeals to young and old because it not only is romantic but is a reminder of how things have changed for the better in their homeland. In the days when farming was the chief occupation, everyone owned his own farm—but they were small farms. To keep the property intact on the father's death, it was always handed on to the oldest son, rather than dividing it among the boys of the family. That left the other sons in the family with nothing, and they often either became priests or emigrated to the Americas. Basques still become priests today, but do so by choice rather than from economic necessity, and there is very little emigration—not even to places as near as Madrid and Barcelona. But the song about *Maite* tells of these earlier times. It is the story of a Basque youth who went to America, and left behind his girl friend, Maite (the Basque name for Maria-Theresa). The young man promised Maite that he would come back and marry her when he had made his fortune in America. Sure enough, he struck it rich and headed for home. But Maite was dead. She had died of a broken heart.

Life in the Provinces

Álava is the largest in size of the three basic Basque country provinces, accounting for about 40 per cent of the region's total area. It is also the most southern and the least populated. At least half of the province's 162,000 inhabitants live in the capital city of Vitoria. Traditionally Álava has been an agricultural province, but industry is growing in importance. There is a plant in Vitoria for the German automobile DKW, and furniture and agricultural machinery are also made there. The Ebro skirts the southern flank of the province, and this area is bursting with vineyards that produce wine with noted names, including an evocative one—Baños de Ebro—which suggests something ideal for champagne baths.

Like all Basques the people of Álava know how to enjoy themselves, and although many of their traditional feasts have a religious base there is plenty of room for merrymaking. *Romerías* ("pilgrimages") usually include picnics and music; and the homeward march, on some occasions, is lighted by torches and the carefree singing and dancing of youngsters through the streets. The traditional *txistu,* a flute-type instrument, is the chief source of music during the August celebrations of the feasts of the Assumption and of St. Roch. The *txistu* used to be made only of wood—often beech—but the makers are beginning to fashion it from modern metal. It still plays the same traditionally lighthearted tune, however.

Of all of Spain's provinces, Guipúzcoa is the smallest. It lies along the Bay of Biscay between the French border and its sister Basque province of Vizcaya. Its population is 540,000. Among its many famous citizens have been world explorer Juan Sebastian Elcano, who was born in 1487 in the fishing village of Guetaria, and St. Ignatius, the founder of the Jesuits (Society of Jesus) who was born a year before the discovery of America in the Loyola *barrio* of the town of Azpetia, 15 miles from Juan Sebastian Elcano's birthplace. Most of the people work in industry, and chemicals, food products, textiles, paper, metals, and plastics are among the things produced. The province is also a significant manufacturer of armament of all types and sizes. In Eibar, a city of 40,000 inhabitants, guns ranging from revolvers to .22s (called "Long Rifles") are made, and many are exported to the United States.

A 16-year-old Barcelona youth, Xavier Yzaguirre, pauses on his way from school to play his flute

Teen-age residents of San Sebastián by the city's harbor

Guipúzcoa's arms industry also produces automatic guns and artillery pieces for NATO.

The province's most dramatic richness is the horseshoe bay which is at the front door of its capital city, San Sebastián. The wide golden beach is always described as the "most beautiful"—in the north, in Spain, in Europe, or in the world, depending on the individual. Santander, next door in Castile, once was the favorite summer place for Spain's royal rulers. Nowadays, San Sebastián is the summertime headquarters of the Spanish government and General Franco has a villa overlooking the San Sebastián beach. San Sebastián has a year-round population of 150,000 but this increases considerably in the summer.

San Sebastián was the first city in Spain (and one of the first in Europe) to have an automatic dial telephone system, establishing it in 1926. The San Sebastián system, although connected with the national service, is still independent, and is operated by the city. Because of an old agreement with Sweden the San Sebastián system is fitted with Swedish equipment while the national company uses accessories and material made in Madrid.

Youth Activities

In winter the young people of San Sebastián spend week nights studying but on the weekend go to a cinema or some place where they can dance. Italian and French films are popular with them when they are not mentally tired because the subjects are complicated and an effort has to be made to understand them. At other times, and particularly in the "exam" season, they take the films as they come—cowboys, James Bond, and the like. There are dancing clubs, called *discotecas* (or, by the French misnomer, *boîtes*), where the entrance fee of 100 pesetas includes a drink—"coke," tonic water, or whatever. It is not necessary to buy a second drink. Girls are not admitted alone to these places but there is no age limit, and girls as young as 14 or 15 are often seen. There are two sessions—one from 7 p.m. to 10 p.m. for the young people, and a later one for the adults. If the young people hear a new record at a *discoteca* which they like, they will all "chip in" to buy a copy. Then, at someone's home, they will learn to play it on their guitars. Many of the young boys and girls play the guitar, and there are singing and dancing evenings at one another's home. Often young Basques from across the border come to visit them and learn the new dances and songs.

School ends late in June just as the summer season begins. Even in the summer most of the young people have to do a bit of early-morning studying, either because they failed some subjects and have to repeat them, or they are preparing for a difficult school year ahead, or they are learning English (or French) on their own. It is 11 a.m. before they get to the beach. The San Sebastián beach is free. If you use a dressing cabin the fee is 5 pesetas, but if you wear your swimming suit under your clothes, no cabin is necessary. Changing into a swimming suit on the beach is not allowed, however. The Basque youths like to swim out to Santa Clara Island, which is 500 to 1,000 yards from the shore depending on the starting point. Getting there first is the idea of everyone—which is typically Basque.

Between swims they play a game called *pala,* using a tennis or plastic ball and a wooden racket. They play it near the water's edge where the hard, firm sand makes it easy for the players to move around swiftly. It is a variety of jai alai. The aim is to bat the ball back and forth without letting it bounce on the ground (no net is used). It is a fast game. Girls play *pala* probably more than the boys. The boys say the girls bat the ball into lazy high flies, and do not slam it in sizzling line drives the way they do.

The young people return home for *almuerzo,* the midday meal, at 2:30 p.m., and then at 4 or 5 p.m. leave for an outing on Mount Igueldo at the western end of San Sebastián's sandy horseshoe. There is a trolley-bus to the foothills of the mountain—a little over a mile from the center of the city—and the fare is only 2½ pesetas, but they think it is more fun to walk. They either take sandwiches with them from home or carry the ingredients for an outdoor meal. The girls usually bring the food (eggs and potatoes, for instance, for the Spanish *tortilla*), but the boys do the cooking. Fish, ham, shrimps, onions, asparagus, or artichokes are sometimes used for the omelette but most prefer the classic tortilla made with boiled potatoes.

Those who belong to the Hippic Club will horseback ride for an hour or two twice a week, and an instructor always goes along. The club membership is 500 pesetas and the monthly dues are quite reasonable —only 50 pesetas. Lessons are a bargain, too—14 pesetas. The young Basques believe the San Sebastián Hippic Club is the least expensive riding club in Europe, and they probably are right.

The Spanish Pittsburgh

The province of Vizcaya has the highest per capita income of any province in Spain ($700.00 a year) and is one of the most densely populated because of its intensive industrialization. Its population (868,000) is the largest by far of any of the provinces of the Basque country, and most of the inhabitants live and work in the general area of Bilbao, the provincial capital.

The river bank of Bilbao, the Spanish synonym for modern industry

Bilbao is known as "Spanish Pittsburgh." It is situated nine miles inland from the sea at the end of the estuary formed by the Nervión River. The left bank of the river, between Bilbao and the open sea, is like one big industrial plant with smokestacks, cranes, and locomotives. The Altos Hornos plant at Baracaldo, halfway between Bilbao and the sea, has been Spain's biggest private steel-producer until now and is currently being modernized with government help as part of the nation-wide steel-expansion program. The iron mines around Bilbao are probably the oldest producing mines in the world. They were put into operation by the Romans and at the end of the last century generated the huge steel mills that have brought Bilbao wealth, fame, and air pollution.

Like England, Spain has five big banks, and two of these originate in Bilbao—the Banco de Vizcaya and the Banco de Bilbao. (The three with central offices in Madrid are Banco Central, Banco Hispano-Americano, and Banco Español de Credit.) In addition to the two big banks, Bilbao has numerous others. The banks are dedicated to the promotion of industry, and one of their greatest projects in recent years

127

was encouraging the establishment of a refinery in Bilbao to treat five million tons of crude oil a year from wells in Libya. In awarding the rights to build and operate the refinery, the government had the choice of proposals from five international groups. In return for the rights, the groups promised such things as low-interest dollar loans to the government, contruction of public-service projects, and help in expanding the tourism industry by building new hotels.

The largest electric utility in Spain, Iberduero, is located at Bilbao. It supplies about 20 per cent of the nation's electric power and is the second largest private company in Spain, the first being the telephone company. The dams of Iberduero are in the central part of Spain, but the company is presently building a thermic plant that will produce electricity from coal and oil in the Greater Bilbao area. This is a more expensive production method, but in Spain where water resources are limited new ways have to be explored. Besides the thermic installation, Iberduero is planning a nuclear plant in the next door Castilian province of Burgos.

Bilbao is approximately 100 miles from the French border, but it seems much further because the roads are not good, and even the train ride can take three hours or more. To encourage the development of tourism in the area and to speed the shipment of materials, an *autopista* ("super-highway") is being planned for completion by 1972. It is a private undertaking and the government is helping to obtain loans from abroad. It will be an expensive project because the terrain is difficult; in addition to crossing the mountains, numerous cities and towns will have to be circumvented. One million dollars a kilometer is the estimate—and there are 170 kilometers on the projected route.

All the industrial hustle and bustle releases various shades of vapors and smokes that lazily float above the river valley and remain there until a strong wind or, more likely, a heavy rain chases them out to sea. Although people talk and complain about the rain they really like it because it clears the air. Clearing the coastal waters is not so easy. The river, which empties into the sea near the beach at Las Arenas, is greatly utilized by the plants along its banks. As a youngster during the Civil War, a local teacher remembers, he and his friends used to hunt for stones at the bottom of the sea along the shores of the Las Arenas beach. Nowadays, he says, young rock-hunters cannot see the bottom.

Like everyone in the Basque country the people of Bilbao enjoy singing, and one of their favorite songs eulogizes some of the things dear to their heart—such as simmering codfish, fried hake, and *chacoli,* a bitterish drink that is somewhere between wine and cider. Youngsters have their own song. For as long as anyone can remember children of Bilbao have been singing the praises of the suspension bridge at the mouth of the river. In Spanish, the youngsters sing-song: "In the whole world there is no suspension bridge more elegant than Bilbao's." It has been a practical bridge, in any case. If it was not for the bridge the people would have to travel nine miles to Bilbao to cross the river. In gondolas, shaped like a trolley car and suspended on cables, they are carried from one side to the other a dozen feet above the water for 1 peseta a crossing. There is talk about building a tunnel, but future generations of Bilbao children will probably still sing about their bridge.

For one peseta, passengers are transported just above the water on the bridge at Las Arenas, a suburb of Bilbao

Students take advantage of the campus of the University of Navarre at Pamplona. Spain's only private university, it is operated by Opus Dei, a Catholic laymen's organization

Navarre and its University

Navarre lies east of the three basic Basque provinces and on the east borders France, with which, in the past, it had strong ties. It is not a large province and the population is only a bit over 400,000. Usually it is grouped with the provinces of the Ebro Valley but it has old links with the Basque country, and some modern ones, too. The newest link is the University of Navarre, which was established in the provincial capital, Pamplona, in 1952, becoming the thirteenth university in Spain and the first private one. It is operated by Opus Dei, a Catholic laymen's organization that was founded in Spain in 1928 and has now spread to more than ·30 other countries. The University of Navarre started with 48 students and six professors, and a decade and a half later had grown to a student body of 6,400 students from 42 nations, a teaching staff of more than 600, and a broad group of schools, including medicine and nursing. There are many nursing schools in Spain but, except for this one, none is attached to a university. The advantage of university attachment is that professors from the medical school can teach some of the courses for the student nurses. In the past year the nursing school has added a special course in psychiatric nursing.

The University of Navarre is generally described as the best university in Spain. Its establishment was especially important to young people of the Basque country because there had been no university in any of their three provinces.

Tuition averages between $80 and $100 a year, depending on the course, but a third of the students are on some type of scholarship and pay from nothing to half what the nonscholarship students pay. Stu-

A furnace for making crystals used in studying metals is among the facilities at the Advanced School for Industrial Engineers, another Opus Dei institution, in San Sebastián

dents living in town can eat in the university cafeteria for 35 pesetas a meal. A typical midday meal consists of a thick *cocido de garbanzos,* a soup of chickpeas (with boiled potatoes added), a large serving of roast veal, a mixed salad, a plate of roasted peppers, a long wheat roll that is as crisp and tasty as a biscuit, an orange from Valencia, and a large glass of wine. Coffee-with-milk costs two pesetas extra, but few order it. Milk or Coca-Cola is also available instead of wine. If the student wishes he can top off the meal with one of the many liquors displayed on the counter behind the cafeteria bar. Spanish brandy is 12 pesetas; a small Scotch Whiskey, 30 pesetas; a "double Scotch," 60 pesetas; and so on. No one seems to order alcoholic drinks at midday and not many do in the evening, either. I asked the woman cashier about the prices for the brandies and whiskies. They are so rarely ordered she had to ask the manager of the bar what they cost.

In Secondary and Technical schools final examination results are usually posted on a bulletin board outside the classroom, but at universities they are given to the students in individual envelopes. At the end of the term the desk of the *conserje* (the "head doorkeeper") in the main hall of the University of Navarre, is encircled by students seeking to know if their "exam" envelope has arrived from their professor as yet. The *conserje* is in charge of distributing the envelopes. After receiving their envelope students leave a gratuity of a few coins in a metal plate on the desk of the *conserje.*

Pamplona

A brass plaque set in the sidewalk of a downtown street in Pamplona marks a critical point in history. The plaque is on the spot where St. Ignatius, at the time a captain in the army of the King of Castile, fell wounded on May 30, 1521, in a battle with the French-supported army of the King of Navarre. While recovering from his wounds at his home in Loyola, Ignatius decided to leave the army and enter the service of Christ. His studies took him to Paris where he met Francis Xavier (Francisco de Javier), a native of the Pamplona area, who had been on the Navarre side during the Castile-Navarre battle. Francis Xavier was a professor of philosophy in Paris at the time of the pivotal battle

132

but some of his brothers were on hand for the fighting. Francis Xavier joined Ignatius in the new Society of Jesus, and subsequently went to the Far East where he became the first of a line of Jesuit missionaries that has never ended.

The newest monument in Pamplona, a statue to Ernest Hemingway, was placed at the entrance to the bullring in the summer of 1968. Hemingway liked Pamplona, and was especially fond of the way the bulls ran through the streets each summer during the festivities honoring St. Fermin, the city's first bishop. The feast used to be celebrated in October, but in 1591 (yes, nearly four centuries ago) the city authorities formally requested the episcopal synod to change the date to July 7 as it would be more convenient. The request was granted, and the new date has been very appropriate to vacationing tourists who throng the city each summer.

Some of the men visitors join in the colorful bull-running which lasts only a couple of minutes but can be quite lively. The bulls doing the running are the six that are to be fought in the afternoon's *corridas*. As a safety factor oxen are mixed in with them, and in addition some of the runners are hand-picked youths who make sure that neophytes do not get in the way of a bull's horns. The bull-running used to be done on horseback, and the lead horseman carried the banner of the city. In the old days, too, the running ended in the main square of the city because in Pamplona, as in most cities of Spain (including Madrid), the Plaza Mayor was the real bull ring until the nineteenth century.

After the bullfights on St. Fermin's feast in Pamplona there is a boisterous street dance, with bands and singing and happy quaffing from the *bota,* the handcrafted Basque wine-skin. Anyone can join the street dancing if they like to dance and have the endurance, but Pamplona women let the men dance by themselves that day. Hemingway described the festivities in *The Sun Also Rises.* The title in Spanish was *Fiesta.* The word *fiesta* is as Spanish as a bullfight. Of all Spaniards the Basques enjoy a bullfight and a fiesta with most vigor.

Galicia and Asturias

The ancient Celts must have brought the weather with them when they migrated to the northwest corner of Spain because Galicia and Asturias, the two regions comprising this part of the Iberian peninsula, are every bit as wet, and vividly green, as Ireland or Scotland. Galicia is the wettest region in all of Spain and the pilgrim city of Santiago de Compostela gets more rainfall than any other community in the nation. If it is not raining the sky is often hidden behind clouds or fog hangs over the countryside. Sometimes the atmosphere is soaked with the *orballo,* a "rain" that is not a rain but more like a soft mist that feels moist when it brushes against your face, but does not dampen anything—least of all the spirits of the people. For the weather is but one reminder of the Celts.

Greek and Phoenician, Swabian and Roman also helped settle the northwest corner of Spain but the surviving characteristic is a happy Celtic lilt in the tempo and temperament of the people of Galicia and Asturias.

The Provinces of Galicia

Sea and mountain seem to vie with each other to dominate the scenery of Galicia which is at the very corner of Spain, facing the Bay of Biscay on the north, the Atlantic on the west, and Portugal on the south. The mountains are numerous, and rise to heights of 6,000 feet in the interior. From its source in the northeast part of the region the Minho heads southward, adding beauty to several cities such as Lugo and Orense before becoming the border with Portugal. But it is the

The cathedral built around the tomb of St. James the Apostle in Santiago de Compostela, Spain's national pilgrimage site

sea which makes the Galician landscape so spectacular. The west coast is fringed with deep, wide *rias*, which are similar to the lochs and firths of Scotland. Galicia is slightly smaller than Catalonia and like it is composed of four provinces: La Coruña, Pontevedra, Orense, and Lugo. The population of the region is close to 3 million.

Capes jutting from the shores of La Coruña province, at the corner of the Iberian peninsula, reach farther north and also farther west than any other part of Spain. General Franco was born in La Coruña at El Ferrol, which is Spain's major naval base and which has been making ships for centuries. Most of the armada used by Philip II was built at El Ferrol. Franco is descended from a family of mariners. His father was in the Navy and a brother, Nicolas, is a retired naval engineer. Because the chief of state was born there the city is now usually referred to as "El Ferrol del Caudillo." The capital city of the province, also named La Coruña, is an important seaport.

Vigo, a busy port in the neighboring province of Pontevedra, has a population of 200,000 and is three times the size of the provincial

A barrel-making workshop in the center of the seaport city of Vigo in Galicia

capital, the city of Pontevedra. Vigo is one of the few places in Spain where trolley cars survive. They are painted a bright white and the windows are piped in crimson.

Most of Lugo, one of the two inland provinces, is spread across a high plateau that is ringed by mountain peaks. The city of Lugo itself, in figuratively the same way, is encircled by a wall which is the best remaining example of the defenses used in Spain by the Romans. A nice thing about the wall is that it is topped by a public passageway similar to the walkway on the wall in the Italian city of Lucca.

The only one of the Galician provinces without a coastline is Orense. It is small and mountainous, and not heavily populated, but is known by wine-drinkers for its vineyards in the Ribeiro district, from which comes a pleasant, not very strong white wine.

Most of the people of Galicia derive their living from farming; fishing is in second place. Industry, with government help, is beginning to develop, but the region as a whole remains poor. The land is often rocky and difficult to cultivate and the mountains force acreages to be split into small parcels. Products caught up in the nets of Galician fishermen are exported throughout Spain as well as to various parts of Europe. Mariscos from Galicia were on the menu of the Spanish Pavilion restaurant at the World's Fair in New York. Even in a fishing center lobster is expensive and on a restaurant menu—where the price is based on weight—it will list for 600 pesetas a kilogram (about $4.00 a pound), on up. The economic law of supply and demand has been forcing prices up in recent years because the lobster catch has been dwindling and consumption keeps rising.

Corn, potatoes, and cabbage are among the main farm products, and cattle-raising is a big activity. The many chestnut trees of the region are useful, and welcome, as feed for pigs—"three centuries to grow, three centuries to exist, and three centuries to die" is what the people say about the hardy chestnut tree. Beef and pork production has given a boost to industry by spawning slaughterhouses, sausage factories, and packing plants.

As a result of the difficulty of making a living at home, Galicians traditionally have migrated. Between 150,000 and 200,000 Galicians

Spanish women are assuming their places in the business world. Preparing for their future in design are these students at the Monte Alegre school in Oviedo

now work in the Common Market countries. In the old days migration was to the Americas—Mexico and Argentina, in particular—but restrictions by the overseas governments have eliminated this outlet, and Galicians now look closer to home for work. In previous migrations to the Americas the whole family usually went along, and they stayed there because, mostly, of the high transportation costs. In the new emigration to the Common Market area only the man of the family makes the trip—it is much cheaper that way—and he returns from his factory job for visits at Christmas and Easter with presents for everyone and enough money to convince family and friends that there are still rich places in the world—and, therefore, hope. Because they come and go so frequently, the modern-day Galician emigrants are known as the *Golondrinas,* the "Swallows."

The massive emigration of the menfolk—then and now—made it necessary for women to step into jobs in industry, on the land, and in

138

the ateliers. It often surprises visitors to see women working every-where. After Madrid and Barcelona, the university at Santiago de Compostela graduates more women doctors than any other medical school in the country. In the fields women work side by side with the men. When the farmer is spraying the potato vines against bugs, the wife walks beside him, holding the line of the spray-gun and the bucket of insecticides. In the late evenings, before the farmer does the milking, the women lead the cattle, like walking a dog, along the grazing lands at the side of the road—the part of the public highway which the Irish call the Long Acre. Two-wheeled carts which are pushed like baby carriages are popular means of transport, especially for rattling cans of milk, but most women still, literally, "use their heads." With nothing but a soiled, wet cloth as a cushion, they carry on their heads huge quantities, such as a bundle of vegetables the size of a bale of hay, or the family wash tumbled into a wicker basket. Women in Galicia are particularly noted for toting tremendous burdens on their heads. When this is pointed out to the men, they laugh and say: "It is good for the figure." But the figures of the women in Galicia are no better, or worse, than those elsewhere in Spain.

Perhaps the most important poet of the nineteenth century was a Galician woman, Rosalia de Castro, who was born in Santiago de Compostela in 1837. Her poetry was suggestive of the sorrows and the

A Galician Miss, cool and casual, in Santiago de Compostela

poverty of the Galicians, of the sadness of the emigrants who had to live beyond their borders. She was known as Our Lady of Saudade—a Portuguese word which means several things together and which add up to "nostalgia and yearning."

The Portuguese language was born in Galicia. In the Middle Ages Galicia reached as far as the Douro River, and until the discovery of the tomb of St. James the Apostle at Compostela the capital was Braga, which is now well within the borders of Portugal. From ancient Galicia the Portuguese language was brought by the Conquistadores to Brazil. The language spoken by the Galician today is more archaic than modern Portuguese, but it is remarkably similar to what the Brazilians speak. Galicians can tune into Brazil on the shortwave radio bands and understand what is being said, but radio broadcasts from Portugal just across the border are practically incomprehensible. *Gallego,* the special language of Galicia, and the way farm people of northern Portugal speak are very much alike. Educated Portuguese, on the other hand, speak a language that has distinctly changed from Gallego. All the people of Galicia speak idiomatic Spanish and 90 per cent of them speak Gallego. In modern times a fair amount of literature in Gallego has been written but the language has not acquired the political implications of Basque or Catalán. Language is a problem in Galicia, nonetheless, because the people would like to have Gallego used—or, at least, taught—in the schools. They would also like wider use of it in their Catholic liturgy. A number of churches have Masses in Gallego, but not many.

The Galicians

The people of Galicia are sentimentalists. They are astute, they like to talk, and they are questioning. A Galician philosopher of three and a half centuries ago, Francisco Sanchez, who was a professor at the University of Montpelier, wrote a book called in Latin *Quod Nihil Scitur,* which in effect meant to say that we know nothing about nothing. Galicians, perhaps, still think this way. They are skeptics. They believe there are many things that modern man, for all his sciences and knowledge, does not know.

140

Of all Spaniards, Galicians are the most superstitious. They still practice superstitions in the fields, especially with fire. The feast of St. John, the midsummer's night of Shakespeare, is a wondrous night when fields are magically sown and the soil is fertilized. They light fires, called *fogueiras* in Gallego, to chase the demons and other evil spirits. Youths sing and dance around the bonfires the whole night through, and at the first light of St. John's day boys and girls prowl along the wooded paths in search of clover leafs. In Scandinavia, in particular, this is a merry time, but in Galicia the adults look upon St. John's eve with awe and pious seriousness. Some communities do not even permit outsiders to attend their observance of the feast. Galicians also are certain that there are people with the gift of the *mal de ojo* (the "evil eye") which, at the will of its possesser, can cause harm to others. The classic emigration of Galicians also figures among their occult habits and beliefs. The formation of the white of an egg, left standing in a bowl over night with water and some herbs, can indicate on the following morning whether a long-absent loved one is still alive or dead. A holy man called St. Martin from Dumio, which is near the present-day Portuguese city of Braga, wrote a book in the sixth century called *De Correctione Rusticorum,* enumerating the superstitions of the Galicians. All the same superstitious rites and beliefs survive.

Death has a special meaning to the Galicians, too. As in biblical times, Galicia still has professional women mourners, the *plañideiras*. They are paid to weep for dead persons, singing a mournful recitation of the good that the person did while he was on this earth. This psalmody changes with each case. Each person has his own *planto*, depending on his profession. The farmer might be eulogized for the way he tended his fields and treated his animals. The *planto* for the barber will recall how carefully he cut the people's hair. The professional mourners exist now mostly in the mountains of Lugo province and are paid relatively well for their services. A group of four earns 250 pesetas and a dinner. The dinner, it is stipulated beforehand, has to include meat.

Galicians are extremely religious, and each village has its sacred patron to whom it prays for help and protection, and whom it honors

once a year with a feast that, besides the religious ceremonies in the church, includes much singing, dancing, and eating. The patron of Vigo is a holy image called Christ of the Salt, who protected the ships that once brought from Andalusia the salt needed to preserve the region's fish and to save its economy. The image is nowadays called Christ-of-the-Victory, perhaps because of the military victory of Franco, a Galician. It could seem to outsiders that the village patrons mean more, or at least are closer, to the people than God Himself. The patron of the region is St. Martin of Tours, and hundreds of churches are dedicated to him. The patron of Spain is St. James the Apostle who is buried in the cathedral of the city named after him, Santiago de Compostela in La Coruña province. St. James, it is believed, came to Galicia after the death of Christ to evangelize the area, and in the Middle Ages his tomb, except for Rome and Jerusalem, became Christianity's most important sanctuary. Many pilgrims still travel the traditional road to

Santiago. In 1965, the most recent Holy Year at the shrine, 1.5 million pilgrims came from all over the world.

The University of Santiago de Compostela

One of the dozen state universities is at Santiago de Compostela. Established in 1533, there are 6,000 young men and women enrolled in the five classic faculties—Philosophy and Literature, Law, Medicine, Pharmacy, and Science. There are also about a thousand students from Latin American countries, including several hundred from Puerto Rico. Santiago's small size (somewhat more than 50,000 inhabitants) helps make it a typical Spanish university city. Santiago has only one public dance hall but most of the social activity takes place in the fifteen colleges (five men's; ten women's), or *colegios mayores*. (The University of Madrid, with an enrollment of 40,000 students, has 60 *colegios mayores*.) The *colegio mayor* is an old Spanish institution where students live and/or eat, attend special lectures, and have dances and parties. During Napoleonic times the *colegios mayores* in Spain's universities were suppressed, but they were revived by the government after World War II. At Santiago most of the students live in boarding-

An aged pilgrim makes her way to the shrine of St. James de Compostela

houses rather than in the colleges because of the limited space, and out of choice as well. This is the way it is in other university cities too. The colleges have only a small number of rooms—100 would be the average—and their main function is to serve as a nucleus for extra-curricular activities.

Santiago students have a reputation for being merry, and bagpipes, a traditional musical instrument of Galicia, join guitars in accompanying songs and dances. The classic student singing group, the *tuna,* is said to have originated in Santiago, and from here spread to other universities. A *tuna* is made up of students dressed in black suits, capes, and hats, who stream long colored ribbons from their shoulders like an exaggerated seal on a royal document. These singing groups perform when and where the mood strikes. At times they serenade outside the windows of the girls' colleges or they might greet a distinguished visitor arriving at the airport or railroad station.

The feast of St. Thomas Aquinas, the traditional patron of students, comes just before the start of spring (March 7) and this fortuitous timing contributes to its merriment. The formal university observance begins the week before the feast with concerts, movies, receptions, and conferences. On the sixth of March, the students with mock solemnity preside at "The Burial of the Sardine," a ceremony in which an iron sardine—a medieval symbol—is laid to rest. The burial takes place at midnight as the students, dressed in pajamas and other night clothes, walk slowly in procession, lugubriously chanting a satirical litany composed in broken Latin. "From the professors," they beseech, "Liberamos, Domine." Free us from girls, from high prices for wine, from cafeteria meals—the requests depend on the season's special gripes. In the early '60s the lighting was increased in the Santiago public park and that year the students, recalling how pleasant the dim *ambiente* used to be for boys and girls on an evening stroll, included municipal authorities in their litany. On the morning of the St. Thomas Aquinas feast the archbishop of Santiago officiates at a Mass in the cathedral, at which the university rector and professors dress in their robes and the senior students wear bright sashes identifying their particular college.

The distinctive barn of the northwest, horreo, *is raised above the ground to protect the contents from moisture and rodents. This* horreo *is typical of Asturias, while the Galicians use smaller ones*

At the front of the cathedral, near the Portico of Glory, is a small statue representing sculptor Maestro Mateo who built the elegant entranceway in the twelfth century. The students have christened the statue "O Santos Dos Croques" ("Saint Tap-on-the-Head"). At exam time they tap the statue's head, and bow. It is their way of recollecting, in the present day, the genius of an ancient artist and to wish for themselves similar intelligence in the examinations facing them.

Asturias

The land of the Astures, a mountainous region nestled on the northern coast between Galicia and Castile is considered the birthplace of modern Spain. In the deep valley of Covadonga, at the eastern end of the region, King Pelayo of the Astures battled the Moors early in the eighth century with his back to the sea and the summits of the Picos de Europa in front. The obscure, savage valley was one of the few patches of land on the Iberian peninsula that had not as yet been seized by the

Moors on their march from the south. The Astures would not budge, fighting among the canyons and cliffs in what might very well have been the first example of guerilla warfare. It was the Moors who withdrew, and the pivotal Battle of Covadonga in the year 718 marked the start of the reconquest of Spain by the Christians. Asturians say that a Virgin appeared to Pelayo at his bivouac near where cool water rolls down the face of the cliffs. She told him to stay, and gave him the courage that brought victory. Five miles away, at Cangas de Onis, Pelayo established the first capital of the kingdom of Asturias, which was the first capital city in Spain.

Covadonga has remained a sacred spot, and has not lost its identity in a labyrinth of villas and boutiques. It consists solely of a mountain, a grotto where the Virgin is venerated, a waterfall, a basilica, a seminary, and a hotel. The buildings are all in the same solid austere Asturian style. The most celebrated residents are the boy choristers who each day sing to the Virgin of Covadonga, the patron of Asturias. A national park in the area also bears the name of Covadonga, and has plants and animals that are no longer seen anywhere else in Spain. The nation's first national park, it was established in 1920 by King Alfonso who liked to come to Asturias for the bear-hunting. Bears still roam the mountains of Asturias—the only area in Spain where they live—and some measure nearly nine feet from nose to tail.

The ancient Astures were a mixture of Celt and Iberian. No one was ever able to dominate them or their descendants. Whenever invaders arrived, the farmers took their cows into the highlands and fought from there. The nearly 100-mile-long chain of mountains at the south serves as a natural protective barrier, even today separating Asturias from Castile. Mountains from the Cantabrian chain form a short distance from the coast and give the region the name "Spanish Switzerland." The western part of Asturias, with its high, empty plateaus, is reminiscent of the steppes of China. An interesting inhabitant is the *urogallo,* a large wild bird that can be hunted only during its 10-day mating season each year—and early in the morning, at that. On these days the bird sings five times, his song lasting a minute each time, as he calls to his mate. While singing he closes his eyes and thus cannot

146

see a hunter approaching for the kill. In the nonmating season the *urogallo* keeps his eyes open, and stays out of the sight of guns and hunters.

Asturias is about one third the size of Galicia. Unlike other regions which consist of many provinces Asturias has only one, Oviedo. Some persons are inclined to refer to the province as well as the region as Asturias. There are 900,000 inhabitants of the region.

The country people live in two-story farmhouses. Bedrooms and the parlor are on the upper floor, while the main floor has the kitchen, a big oven at one side of the kitchen for baking bread, and a courtyard somewhat similar to those in Dutch and Flemish farm dwellings where the family cow and pigs are kept. Farmhouses of the northwest are noted for their unique grain-storage places which are wooden structures raised on stilts several feet above the ground to protect them against dampness and field mice. The ones in Galicia are small while those in Asturias are as big as a one-car garage.

Oviedo leads the other provinces of Spain in the production of milk, cattle, and apples. From the apples Asturians make *sidra* ("cider"),

The art of serving cider, a favorite beverage of the Asturians, is carefully executed at this café in Oviedo

which is a popular drink at *aperitivo* time, and the way it is served provides *divertissement* for everyone in the café. A waiter holds a glass, slightly tilted, in one hand, and with the other pours cider from a bottle that is two to three feet above the glass. An expert rarely lets a drop splash onto the floor. The unusual manner of serving causes air to circulate through the cider, improving its taste. It is a traditional farmer's version of the modern aeration process now used in some United States communities for making drinking water more palatable. The cider glasses in Asturias are five-inch crystal beakers with a three-inch diameter, and cost much more than the liquid they hold. The price of a quart bottle of cider at a popular bar in downtown Oviedo, the capital city, is 12 pesetas.

The Industrial Triangle

Asturias is also the leading producer of steel, zinc, aluminum, and coal. Its coal mines traditionally have accounted for three quarters of the total output in Spain, and this is the source of the problem facing the Asturian economy today. The winds of change have reduced the use of coal. Butane gas has replaced it domestically and the railroads in Asturias, once a big customer, are now almost completely electrified,

The new steel plant in Avilés, in Asturias

while the nonelectrified ones rely on diesel oil. The trend against the use of coal is recognized both by the national government and the coal miners, and plans are being made to turn the coal economy, by the mid '70s, into one that is based on steel.

This means that 35,000 of the present 45,000 coal miners will have to be retrained for jobs in steel plants that are now being built, and in auxiliary industries. The dramatic transformation not only calls for changes in the region's economic system but in the personal lives of 15,000 families. From small dreary towns in the southern part of Asturias the miners will be uprooted and brought to new homes and jobs along the coast. The mass movement will not be without tension. Asturias has always been a politically sensitive spot, and this might be one reason why the government has made it a major target for investments. Men who risk their lives daily by going underground to dig out its coal have few inhibitions and fewer fears. The revolution of 1934, the social revolt which rocked Spain, was practically started by Asturian miners who stormed into the city of Oviedo from the mining district and set fire to the university and other buildings.

Because of the tremendous capital investments Asturias is expected to become the most important industrial center in the north. The keystone of the investment and development area will be the triangle formed by the city of Oviedo on the south, fifteen miles from the sea, and the coastal cities of Avilés, at the west, and Gijón, on the east. Gijón with a population of 160,000 is already slightly larger than the provincial capital. The Musel harbor at Gijón, separated from the beach area by a convenient cape, is being enlarged to handle super-tankers and large cargo ships. A total of 3,500 million pesetas is being invested to make Gijón the main shipping point in the north. Many new apartment houses are being built along the beachfront between the Yacht Club and the 15-year-old Isabella-the-Catholic Park. (Gijón people are proud of the black swans in the park lake and the statuary group, nearby, featuring Bambi, Snow White, and the Seven Dwarfs, which was dedicated by the children of Gijón to Walt Disney in the summer of 1968.) A typical three-bedroom apartment, with a living room, dining room, and kitchen in one of the new shoreside buildings costs 400,000 pesetas.

Plans for transforming Asturias into a major steel-producing area originated two decades ago when the total steel production in the nation was less than one million tons a year. The Ministry of Industry, looking to the future, asked private industry and financial institutions in 1950 to draft a steel-expansion program. Everyone was willing, but the nation still was nursing political, economic, and social sores from the Civil War, and private financial means did not exist to do anything about boosting steel production. The government therefore decided to form a company, Empresa Nacional Siderúrgica de España, S.A.—Ensidesa, as it is known acronymistically—which would build a huge plant in the small coastal town of Avilés and spearhead the national steel program of the future. In the late '50s enough capital was rounded up from commercial and savings banks, and from other sources, to make it possible for the government to put its steel-expansion program into operation. Along the shoreline of Avilés, where nothing existed two decades ago, Ensidesa has built on reclaimed land a half-billion-dollar seven-mile-long plant that already produces two million tons of steel a year and will double that output by 1970.

Production at the Avilés plant alone will account for 4 million of the 10 to 12 million tons of steel that the government expects will be needed annually in the '70s.

Two other projects, which like Avilés are receiving government aid, will provide the bulk of the remaining needs. One project involves the creation of a mixed private-public company by three veteran steel producers of the region whose combined annual output has been about 500,000 tons. Duro Felguera, one of these three companies, is almost a century old, and the two others are not much younger. The three old-timers have no plans to move from their familiar working places and have chopped away a mountain at Serin, five miles west of Gijón in the direction of Avilés, to make a brand-new site for the plant of the new company which will be known as Union Nacional Industrias Siderúrgicas de Asturias (UNINSA). The UNINSA plant will be electronically operated and as modern as any in the world. The first stage of production is to reach 1.7 million tons a year by 1970 and 2.4 million two years later.

The third steel-expansion project calls for modernization of the Altos Hornos complex in Bilbao which now has a 25 per cent participation of Armco Steel Company of Pittsburgh. The current annual production of the Basque plant is 1 million tons, and this is to climb to somewhere between 2.7 and 3 million in 1970.

Output from the two projects in Asturias (Avilés and UNINSA) combined with the new production level at Altos Hornos will provide about 9.5 million of the 10 to 12 million tons of steel anticipated by the government as the annual requirement in the '70s. Some steel men believe the government's estimate is on the high side. But if it is not, there is a possibility that an additional half million tons can be squeezed out of the present capacity. The government, still thinking in terms of 12 million tons, is making a study to see whether it will be necessary to build a fourth plant—possibly in neighboring Galicia's La Coruña province. That would make the northwest the undisputed steel capital of Spain.

Building a New Way of Life

The coastal town of Avilés is a fascinating example of what the transformation from coal to steel means for Asturias. Avilés used to be the kind of town that the late Palacio Valdes, the novelist, wrote about in *La Aldea Perdida* ("The Lost Village"). He told of a family who migrated to the Americas, made money, and, because Asturians never forget their native region, returned home to settle down in a small village and quietly tally their stocks. Avilés was a community of *cuentarentistas* ("coupon-cutters"), a very proper place where everyone lived tranquilly, were somewhat older than Spaniards in other towns, and were proud of the Cultural Center with its library and lecture hall. In the early '50s its population was somewhere between 12,000 and 15,000. Now there are that many people on the steel company's payroll, and the population has soared to 80,000. It is expected that this figure will double in the early '70s, giving Avilés a growth record that cannot be matched by any other city in Spain.

By building a housing development that is equipped with everything from schools and a church to a swimming pool and *frontón*, the steel

Progressive education in Asturias: the traffic safety and training school in Gijón, where streets are designed to resemble those of a city

company has cushioned the transformation for the townspeople and for its employes. There is also a shopping center which sells food and clothes for the whole family at cost. Three thousand apartments are in the development, the average one having three bedrooms, a dining room, a living room, kitchen, and bath. Most impressive of all is the symbolic rent of 50 pesetas a month. One area of the development is set aside for the workers; another for shop stewards; and another for administration chiefs, while the company executives live in villas and apartments in Avilés.

Employes interested in buying their own homes can do so with their employer giving great assistance. A few miles from the steel plant a private firm has built 5,000 houses in a subdivision it has christened La Luz ("the Light"), and the steel company has bought 2,200 of the units for resale to its employes on special terms. The down payment is 40,000 pesetas and the steel company will advance this to an employe without interest. The monthly payment for one of these three-bedroom houses is 500 pesetas which includes all charges, and it is estimated that a worker can own his own home in eight or nine years with the normal schedule of payments.

The low-cost housing and the nonprofit shopping center add greatly to the purchasing power of the monthly wages, which average between 6,000 and 8,000 pesetas. There are other fringe benefits. Electricity, water, and coal are free. A clinic with 13 doctors, three operating rooms, specialists on call, a blood bank, and an oxygen supply is ready to serve the whole family. Sisters of Charity serve as nurses in the clinic and teach in the girls' school (first grade through high school). The Salesians of Don Bosco teach the boys.

A young Asturian executive at the steel plant observes that an odd thing about the character of his fellow people is that they can do great things abroad, when they migrate to places like South America, but till now have done little at home.

"Asturias," he points out, "is rich in natural resources—coal, iron, and plenty of rivers to produce electricity. Anywhere else in the world if you have these three things, you can do everything. But until now the people of Asturias have been sleeping. I cannot understand why the parents who had a chance to travel and study abroad, and see things, have not done more here with the resources that are available."

The new generation of Asturians seems to be making up for lost time.

Portugal Above the Tagus

If the Tagus River after entering Portugal from the plateau of Castile followed a straight path to the sea, instead of veering southward, it would cut the country exactly in two. Although it seeks to evade the responsibility of being a boundary line, the Tagus does effectively divide Portugal into northern and southern halves which are almost alike in population, but distinctively different in topography, in the character of the people, and in the way of life.

The north of Portugal—the area above the Tagus—is crowded with mountains and highlands which leave very little room for valleys to spread out and not much in the way of cultivable land. Only about a third of the entire area is at a low enough level so that crops can be grown, but the soil is fertile. The farmlands are speckled with wheat fields, fruit orchards, vegetable gardens, and olive groves, and there are many dairy-farmers and cattle-raisers. The most distinguished agricultural product is the group of wines which range from the anonymous ones that, instead of water, are put on family dinner tables throughout the area to the princely port which has found its way into the nation's name and into the crystal glasses of wine connoisseurs everywhere.

The farmers of the north, unlike the vast majority of those who work on the lands south of the Tagus, are their own bosses, owning the farm which gives them and their families a living. But their domain does not stretch far beyond the front door of the farmhouse, often being no more than an acre or two. Throughout Portugal there are over three quarters of a million pieces of property and the majority of these are north of the Tagus, parceled out for the most part into the coastal section. Even

View of Oporto looking across the Douro River from the left bank. In the fore-ground is the Luis I double-decker bridge

the vineyards are spread out among thousands of different owners—
and the people like it that way, preferring to rely on themselves and
to be independent. Their feeling of independence is so strong that they
even shun cooperatives although they are aware that such communal
organizations can reduce production costs and raise output. The people
of northern Portugal are a lot like their rugged mountains.

Traditionally industry has been centered in the coastal strip but
national development programs are pushing it continuously further into
the mountains. Although textiles remains the main industry, the industrial horizon is broadening all the time and the young Portuguese of
today starting out on his first job is likely to be on the payroll of a
brand-new plastics, electronics, or automobile-assembly plant rather
than an old-time cotton or fish-canning company. An active reforestry
program is cloaking the bleak sides of mountains with eucalyptus trees
and more than a third of the area above the Tagus consists of forests.
The forest lands feed paper and pulp plants and provide work for the
young people who no longer want to stay down on the farm, and are
lured by factory jobs and city life.

Along the coast the weather, winter and summer, is mild as a general
rule, and on some Christmas Days roses are often still in bloom. Snow
is a rarity but it does sometimes fall, and when it does it brightens the
landscape and adds a sparkle to conversations. In the mountainous
interior, temperatures reach the classic peaks of continental summers
and winters. The Atlantic beaches are crowded with sun-bathers and
not so much with swimmers, because the ocean waters of the north
never really get warm. Fog frequently hems in the coast like a mountain
wall in the summer and in winter curls up river valleys.

The north is extremely active in cultural matters, with many lectures,
conferences, and other intellectual endeavors sparked by the universities in Coimbra and Oporto and by the university-level Faculty of
Philosophy of Braga, a Jesuit undertaking. Businessmen and professional men assist in sponsoring visits by foreign scholars and international personalities to give talks on music, art, and other subjects
ranging across the intellectual spectrum. Music tastes are high, and noted
concert artists appear regularly in Oporto and other cities of the north

A farm woman on the highway near the village of Fatima

under sponsorship of local private subscription groups. Much of the cultural activity in Oporto is due to the Ateneu Comercial, a private organization founded by businessmen in the nineteenth century, which arranges free conferences, music programs, and art expositions.

As in Spain, the principal and main social unit is the family, which is presided over by the paterfamilias. The woman is responsible for the day-to-day raising of the children but the father of the family keeps himself continuously informed of what his boys and girls are doing, and are planning to do, and if he does not approve makes his view known at once. The opinion of the father, once it is announced, settles any issue that had been under discussion in the family. Boys and girls might be in the same class as the children next door but their parents might never meet, except on the stairway. An invitation to the home of a Portuguese family comes—if it ever does—only after a person has been scrupulously regarded from a distance for a long time.

The Tagus is by no means the only river of the north. The word "Foz" is repeated so often on a map of the coast—Foz do Rio Minho,

157

Foz do Rio Douro, Foz do Rio Mondego, and so forth—that one might think it meant "lighthouse," instead of identifying the mouth of such-and-such river. The Douro roars into Portugal in dramatic cascades after tumbling hundreds of feet from the Castilian *meseta*. Portugal and Spain have saddled the Douro basin with dams they operate cooperatively, and those on the Portuguese side create two thirds of the electricity used in Portugal.

Another Iberian river with a Spanish heritage, the Minho, comes down from Galicia to form the border between Spain and Portugal before vanishing in the Atlantic. Often sandbanks loom just below the water's surface like the glossy skull of a man that is going bald. The shallowness of the river conveniently takes place at points where trees on each bank try to reach over to the other side, and this facilitates the smuggling of foreign cigarettes, transistor radios, and other articles viewed by the purchasers as necessities and by the tax men as luxuries.

The Northern Provinces

Six of Portugal's eleven provinces fit completely within the upper half of the country, and the Minho River has given its name to the one which is physically at the northwest corner and is symbolically the cornerstone of the Portuguese nation. No section of Portugal is older than Minho province and none has been populated longer. The first king of Portugal was born in Guimarães and he was crowned by the archbishop of Braga who bears the title of "Primate of all the Spains," because his see was reconquered from the Moors even before Toledo. Minho people are known as hard workers. In water up to their knees they drag the ocean bottom for seaweed, raking it in like treasure, and spreading it along the beach to dry so that it can be sold as fertilizer or for the making of agar-agar. In small workshops furniture, embroideries, laces, and linens are made and then brought to one of the province's many weekly fairs to be put on the open market. Cabbage, in soup or on a plate with potatoes, is a staple of the Minho diet, and it is accompanied by the fresh *vinho verde* which is less alcoholic than other wines.

Trás-os-Montes fills the northeast corner of Portugal which—just as its name says—is behind the mountains. Each of its four sides is a granite wall and at the southern end the Douro systematically gnaws an ever-deeper gorge among the peaks and mountain spurs. Like all great wines, port is produced in the valley of a river. The upper Douro Valley is its home, and the high mountains shelter the vineyards against cold winter winds.

At Miranda do Douro, on a plateau nearly a mile high, one can look across the border to Spain. The people of Miranda have their own language—not Portuguese, not Spanish—but one which seems to have proceeded on its own directly from Latin. Some say it is Basque; the people of Miranda call it Mirandese.

Here in the province of Trás-os-Montes, with mountains blocking the way to the sea, is the birthplace of Magellan. On a somewhat lesser scale other people from the province have explored the New World, and the greater part of the Portuguese immigrants to the United States have come from Trás-os-Montes. It is not unusual, near the water fountain of a village, to encounter an aged bronzed man who speaks English —and who might even be an American citizen. In the area above the Tagus are more than 1,500 Portuguese-Americans who either became naturalized citizens in the United States, or were born there of immigrant parents, and have returned in their old age to their native land.

The Beira Alta, a lonely, long province encircled by mountains, flanks Spain, but this proximity does not at all mean easy communications. Crossings are few and infrequent, and one at the north follows such a twisting-and-turning route that the mountain people good-humoredly refer to it as "The Excommunicated Way."

Guarda, more than a half mile high in the mountains, is one of the highest cities in Europe. Its houses are made from the same austere granite which marks the landscape, and slate is used for roofs as well as for barn floors. Shepherdesses in long, hooded capes as black as the darkest members of their flocks stand silent and contemplative while the sheep hunt for something to eat among the outcrops of mossy stones. The most celebrated shepherd in the province's history is Viriathus who led the people in resisting the Romans. He is now remembered with a monument near Viseu where he had staked out his camp.

The word Baixa ("low") in the province name of Beira Baixa obviously refers to its geographical relationship to its sister province, Beira Alta, rather than to the topography, because it, too, is a mountainous area. The high-level Serra da Estrela slashes diagonally across the northern part of the province and the mountain city of Covilhã, fast becoming a center for factory jobs, cherishes its ancient privilege of providing the cloth used in uniforms of the Portuguese army.

Olive oil, the famous product of Castel Branco, adds substance and flavor to thick vegetable soup which sometimes is fortified with chunks of pork. The people traditionally have welcomed the poorest of strangers to share their food with them—no matter how little there is. But before a stranger sets off on his journey again he may be solemnly urged to keep an eye out, especially late in the day, for ancient Moorish princesses, for the wandering souls of the long departed, or even for the Devil himself and his cohorts who might be lurking at the roadside.

The coastal province of Beira Litoral is the spiritual center of Portugal containing—all within relatively few miles from one another—the

A windmill in the fields of central Portugal, not far from Leiria

University of Coimbra, the tomb of the Unknown Soldier at Batalha, and the sanctuary of Fatima.

Spiritual and Intellectual Center

The tomb of the Unknown Soldier is housed in a massive monument raised by King John I in the fourteenth century to commemorate a pivotal victory over the Castilians and was dedicated to Santa Maria de Vitoría (Our Lady of Victory). Until the early part of the nineteenth century it was a monastery—and a big one!—with five cloisters. Part of the building is now used as a parish church. Two soldiers stand guard continuously in the dimly lighted columnless chamber where the Unknown Soldier is buried and although it is a large high-ceilinged room the acoustics are eerily perfect. Portuguese visitors like to go to a far corner and hum a note or two of their national hymn and awe their friends, and themselves, with the clear way in which their voice fills the vast space. The Batalha monument is not far from the city of Leiria, the district capital with a population of 10,000.

In the center of Leiria is a hill crowned by a castle that Alphonse I built in the twelfth century in the early days of Portugal's history. There is a panoramic view of Leiria from the top of the castle, a favorite rendezvous of Portuguese people. They are not so much interested in the view but in seeing the top-floor room where special state banquets are held on extraordinary occasions, such as the official visits of General Franco and Haile Selassie some years ago, and they amuse themselves in speculating about the difficulties in getting the food, and the VIP guests, up the steep, tortuous pathway. The Leiria castle makes a romantic backdrop for the young country girls in a Domestic Sciences school which is in a direct line with it a few hundred yards away. At sunset the girls sit in the school garden, with a transistor radio turned low, and contemplate the castle as they sew and chat. Seventy-five girls in their late teens attend the school's three-year course, and all come from small rural villages. The school was started by the Leiria Catholic Action director in the early '50s to help raise the standard of living of country people. Social workers were reluctant to leave their homes and families to work in mountain villages so the country girls were brought to the city. The school trains the girls who will return to their villages and teach others—young and old—about family life, taking care of a house, and the like.

The favorite lookout point for the people of Coimbra is the Penedo da Saudade, a pine-filled bluff, criss-crossed with casual paths. Aged men and women, young people from the university, nursemaids with babies, school girls—in short, all Coimbra—like to sit here in the afternoon and gaze upon their city. Just below is the Mondego, which during the summer the people derisively call a "sandy road" because it is so dry that women can walk out to the center of the broad river bed to wash the family clothes in a pool of water that looks as though it was left over from a nasty thundershower. On the far bank is a large cloister-like building, once a convent of the Poor Clares and now a military casern. Nearby in a smaller building, with a smokestack poking above its tiled roof, textile workers make a well-known cloth, called Santa Clara. Behind these buildings is *Portugal dos Pequenitos,* Young People's Portugal, a magic wonderland of several acres, filled with miniature representations of typical houses, monuments, and farms from each of the nation's provinces. Routes pioneered by Portuguese explorers to far-off lands, from the Azores to India, are traced on a large map. "And if greater was the world, greater would be the Portuguese maritime discoveries," is written about the map, simultaneously echoing the ancient words of Camões and the moody thoughts of today's Portuguese. Just behind the Penedo da Saudade is a huge convent where Sister Lucy, the only survivor of the three Fatima children, lives the cloistered life of a Carmelite; and spread across a nearby hill is the Coimbra University complex.

The University of Coimbra has been a center of the nation's intellectual life since its founding in 1290, and it evokes nationwide memories and nostalgia. Its alumni range from Camões to Salazar, and in the million-volume library is the original manuscript of the Portuguese epic by Camões, *Os Lusíadas.*

Nowadays, most of the 8,000 students come from the north. They pay a tuition that averages 1,400 escudos a year, but medical students pay a third more than that. The students live with families and in

This wide stairway leads to the University of Coimbra on a hill overlooking the city

boardinghouses and give a youthful air to this ancient city. Customs are almost as old as the university, and are as carefully followed as an order of the rector. The most rigorous customs apply to the men students, apparently because women have been admitted only in relatively recent times.

In the first year, men cannot even have a briefcase, and must carry their books and papers with a strap or under their arm. In the second year a briefcase is permitted but it must not be folded even if it is empty. Permission to fold the briefcase comes in the third year. In the fourth year students can tack onto the briefcase a small strip of colored ribbons identifying the faculty in which they are studying. Students studying at Coimbra for a fifth year let this hesitant piece of silk expand into wide, long banks that stream from their important briefcases. Each faculty has its special color. Law is red; medicine, yellow; philosophy and literature, dark blue; engineering, brown, mathematics, light blue and white; pharmacy, violet; and agronomy, green and white.

*Students at the University
of Coimbra wear traditional
black capes*

The classic attire of the male student is black cape with matching trousers, and a white shirt. The origin of this seemingly somber, but actually elegant, garb is that in times past most of the students were priests and they dressed in black. All the capes, even the newest ones, are frayed at the bottom, with strips of cloth of different lengths hanging like woolen stalactites. There are two principal theories about this tattered look. The students like to say that each of the frayed strips represents a romance. Others say that the woebegone bottom of the student capes is a reminder of the days when the oldest son in the average Portuguese family inherited all the property and, being rich, did not have to go to the university. His younger brothers attended the university, and being poor did not have the money to buy a new cape when the old one wore out. Tattered and torn capes were the style out of necessity, but by choice have remained in fashion.

The entertainment of the university students is built around a guitar and the *fado*. *Fados* are songs about events, experiences, people—the marvelous range of life. At Coimbra the romance of the *fado* is heightened when it is sung by a group of students in traditional university capes.

The Village of Fatima

The village of Fatima, where three shepherd youngsters in 1917 reported that a beautiful lady appeared to them and said she was the Mother of God, is still so remote from the rest of the world that the railroad station serving it is 15 miles away. The station is at Chão de Maçãs ("Ground of Apples Trees") but this is too formidable a name for visiting pilgrims to pronounce so the name Fatima is used. Apple trees, if they ever did flourish in the zone, have vanished and the

A newly married couple leaves the basilica of Fatima commemorating the vision of the three shepherd children over a half century ago

ground is covered with small stones which the railroad draws upon as track ballast. Pope Paul VI, in one of his famous air trips, journeyed to Fatima in 1967 and a million pilgrims joined him at the shrine. Some Portuguese from northern villages walk to Fatima, and foreigners meeting them along the road are inclined to think they are too poor to buy a train or bus ticket. However, they walk either to thank Our Lady of Fatima for having answered their prayers or to encourage her to help them with their special petition. Some pilgrims travel the last mile to the sanctuary on their knees.

A number of pilgrims walk a mile and a half to the tiny hamlet of Aljustrel where the three little shepherds were born, hoping to catch a glimpse of Lucy's sister and the brother and sister-in-law of the dead Jacinta and Francisco. What surprises many is that Aljustrel is just like any other hamlet of the north, with small houses lining a short, narrow, dirt road that is the main street and with pigpens and vegetable gar-

Like many other pilgrims, a young Portuguese boy "walks" around the shrine of Fatima on his knees

dens tucked into the spaces between houses. Women wear big black scarves on their head, folded tightly back like the head coverings some fashion models use to protect their hair on the way to the photographer's studio. Relatives of the Fatima shepherds look and act like other adults of the hamlet, and their children and grandchildren look and play like other youngsters.

Aljustrel is one of 25 hamlets depending on the parish church at Fatima. They are small hamlets of a few hundred people, and are spread across an area that fans out from the church several miles in every direction. It is a parish of 1,300 families—6,000 residents in all. Fifty years ago 400 families lived in the parish. Potatoes, fruits, wheat, and olives fill the fields, and the people live from what they grow. Their olives, the villagers of Fatima say, produce the most pure oil in Portugal. The production of olive oil has good and bad years. In good years, the people live well, and can buy beef or even fish for some of the meals during the month. In bad years, potatoes is the main dish rather than an accompaniment.

The parish church is dedicated to St. Anthony, and this is one of the year's big feasts. The Portuguese are quick to point out to foreigners that the friar was born in Lisbon although he died in Padua. As in the early liturgy of the Church, the farm people bring offerings of bread, money, oil, and wine on St. Anthony's feast for the support of their parish church and for distribution to the poor. Oxen drawing wagonloads of bread and other gifts circle the church in a solemn procession and children happily wear the new coats, dresses, and outfits they had asked their parents to get them for St. Anthony's feast. After the morning services in the church the people spend the rest of the day on the church grounds in a parish party, sharing with other families the pieces of chicken and pork, strips of bacon, fish fillet, tomatoes, and homemade cakes they had carried from home.A volunteer band plays music for the singing of familiar songs and *fados,* and at the edge of the crowd young people dance to the music of a transistor radio and concentrate on learning the English words of a brand-new song from the United States or England. Devout people bring bread to the feast as an offering, often to fulfill a vow or promise they made to the saint when they were sick. The bread is blessed during the services in the church and part of it remains on the altar to be used as consecrated bread. The rest is distributed to the people as a souvenir of the feast. Some people eat the bread and others, believing it is good against moths, take it home and put it in their closets.

Oporto

Douro is the smallest of Portugal's provinces, even though it possesses the metropolis of Oporto. At Avanca, a small town between Coimbra and Oporto, the walls of the railroad station are tiled with figures of ox-carts and of women carrying amphoras of water and of oil on their head. Today's setting is not too much different from the one represented in the station's *azulejos*. The country women have a way of looping a large shawl around their shoulders and under their arm so that, like a hammock, it supports the baby they are holding with one hand and leaves the other free for carrying bundles. The blouses and skirts of all of them are of dark shades, black being the favorite color. Many go barefoot to save shoe money for food. Smokestacks rise in the fields like exclamation points emphasizing that industry is now lending a helping hand to the province's economy. Along the coast fishermen still sail off each spring to bring back from the banks of Newfoundland the codfish that Portuguese like so much and which the women can prepare in dozens of mouth-watering ways. The voyage in search of this prized fish is a perilous one and the women don black shawls, like widows, when their men folk cast off and do not doff them until they return safely in the fall.

The people of Lisbon say that they live in the first city of Portugal, that there is no second, third, or fourth city, and that the fifth city in the nation is Oporto. There is a spirited north-south rivalry beween Lisbon and Oporto. The people of Oporto never hesitate to explain the difference between the north and the south. "We are descended from the Celts and from the Romans," a visitor might be told. "In the south they are all Moors." The Douro and Minho provinces comprise the old-time County of Portucale which got its name from the ancient

A train passenger at Valenca da Minho, in northern Portugal at the Spanish border, presents a typical picture of the Portuguese country woman

settlement, now Oporto, near the mouth of the Douro River. (Mariners from Gascogny in the tenth century called the settlement, in French, Porte de Cale, "Gateway of the Inlet.") The County of Portucale, after it declared its independence from the Spanish king, spread south as the Moors were progressively routed and in its expansion acquired full nationhood and the name Portugal. (Mexico City is the only other world metropolis which has given its name to a nation.) The name Oporto in Portuguese is actually Porto. In using the word Portuguese employ the article (O Porto), and this is the only case in which they do so with the name of a town. When English visitors generations ago constantly heard Portuguese refer to the city as "O Porto," they assumed it was one word, and began spelling its name as Oporto.

Oporto is on the right bank of the Douro, a half dozen miles from the river's mouth. It is opposite Vila Nova de Gaia, where the port-wine shippers have their lodges. It is estimated that one out of seven people of Oporto depend directly or indirectly on the port-wine industry. The wine is carried by barge downriver from the vineyard area to the lodges of the shippers where it is kept in casks, and bottled only when ready for sale or shipment. There are about 60 wine shippers, and of these perhaps a dozen are quite large. In summer tourists may visit one of the firms to sample a free glass of the famous wine on its home grounds.

Oporto climbs up a high hill at the edge of the Douro and its major monuments, such as the cathedral and the bishop's palace, form most of its wide, lofty façade. Like the single candle on the birthday cake of someone who does not wish to disclose her age the Torre dos Clérigos, Portugal's highest tower, accents the skyline. From the looks of the skyline it might seem that only Catholic churches are in Oporto. Actually, there are a number of non-Catholic places of worship, including a beautiful synagogue and Baptist, Methodist, and other Protestant churches.

At some points on the shore stairs lead to the water and the Douro is used as the basin for the family wash by housewives who live in the crusty houses along the alleys that unwind from the cathedral. While

A downtown café in Oporto, a popular stopping-place, but mostly for men

their mothers do the washing children cavort on the river bank as if they were in a public playground, and the playing children and the parents laughing and talking with one another give the impression that washday is the happiest day in the week. Near the Don Luis I double-decker bridge the port area limits the drying space for the women's wash, and they have to hang it from their windows. But a mile or two downriver they can string lines between the trees on the shore. Steep streets lead from the water to the center of the city, and the granite used in the buildings and the narrowness of the streets cloak the downtown area in a gray that can look grim even on a sunny day.

The population of Oporto, including its suburbs, is close to 700,000. There are restaurants of all price ranges and cafés which spill onto the sidewalk. The cafés, during the day as well as in the evening, are patronized primarily by men. Women rarely step into them—and then only when accompanied by a man. Chairs and small tables, often trimmed in silver, are arrayed in long lines across the coffee-house floor and as each new patron arrives a waiter in a spotless white jacket and black tie approaches ceremoniously to take the order. Ninety-nine times out of a hundred the order is for a small cup of black coffee that costs one and a half escudos but the waiter acts as if he was prepared to be asked for anything from Postum to yoghurt. At breakfast and at teatime the waiter brings to the table a plate of cupcakes, rolls, and pastry—unless the patron indicates beforehand that he does not wish anything to eat. A fixed number of items is on each plate and the waiter, when calculating the bill, mentally notes how many have disappeared but he asks the patron, nonetheless, to tell him the number he has eaten. Like the city's busdrivers, the café waiters of Oporto wear protective cuffs on their sleeve. This custom is not followed in Lisbon.

Small, neighborhood bars serve cabbage soup, slivers of fried codfish, portions of rice and even full meals, and many men spend the early evening in these places, watching television or playing cards with cronies. The wine they drink is a local one that costs only an escudo or two a glass. They drink port only on special occasions because even in the wine's frontyard it is expensive. If a family is dining out—and for the average family that would be a special event—they do so usually on

171

Sundays, and the wife studies the menu before ordering as carefully as a parking ticket.

At home as well as in restaurants tripe is often on the menu, and the people of Oporto are known as tripe-eaters, bearing the title with great pride. They say the designation originates with the way their ancestors voluntarily butchered and salted all their cattle to provision the expedition undertaken against the Moors at Ceuta by the city's most famous native son, Prince Henry the Navigator. All they kept for themselves was the tripe, but in the process they gained an enduring reputation.

Celebrating the Past and the Future

Oporto's most distinguished adopted son is Vimara Peres who, eleven centuries ago, was given the mission by the king of Asturias of reconquering the district from the Moors. Presumably because his mission was carried out so long ago little has been written about him, and there are only three or four lines relating to his key exploit in an ancient manuscript in the national archives in Lisbon. But amends have been made and a splendid equestrian statue, inscribed with his name and the dates 868-1968, now stands in the square in front of the cathedral.

Shoeshining operations at a series of impromptu stands in downtown Oporto

Modern-day Oporto follows the Douro right to the sea, and it is hard to say exactly where its boundaries end and those of the oceanside city of Matosinhos begin. Matosinhos itself is having its own boom. For a long time sardine-canning has been the leading industry at Matosinhos, and there are several dozen factories. Portugal's sardines rank with the best that any nation fishes out of the Atlantic, and the amount taken off Matosinhos accounts for more than half of the total Portuguese catch. Even bigger things are in store. The harbor is now being expanded into what will be one of Europe's largest ports and the first oil refinery of the north is scheduled for completion by 1972. That will be something to celebrate.

People of the Douro are always celebrating.

St. John the Baptist's feast is a legal holiday in Oporto, and other towns of the Douro declare a holiday in the same way on the feast day of their patron. Religious feasts are the bases of many of the celebrations in Oporto and the neighboring localities but there are also many fairs—cattle, vegetable, ceramics, and iron among others—which are the source of general amusement. At Amarante, twice a year, old maids and bachelors ask Saint Goncalo to aid them in finding a marriage partner.

There are few bullfights in the north and none at all in Oporto, but Póvoa de Varzim, a beach resort near Oporto, frequently arranges some during the summer. Newspapers in July and August run long lists of festivals, fairs, folk-dancing exhibitions, and fireworks displays, like a movie schedule in a weekend American newspaper. They are family attractions that cost little or nothing except for the incidental sums one pays for such things as fried sardines, a glass of green wine, a paper cup of ice cream, a bowl of soup, or a roll crammed with serra cheese.

The people of Oporto and its small province have a saying that there is no Sunday without a festival, no heart without love, and no house without devotion.

INFANTE
D HENRIQUE

Lisbon and the Land Below the Tagus

A foreigner who lives at Sagres at the southwest tip of the Iberian peninsula told a visitor one afternoon not long ago why he chose for his home this beautiful, sunny but, nonetheless, remote point of land that is nearly 200 miles south of Lisbon. "The Portuguese will never build any of those big hotels here or turn it into a tourist resort," the foreigner explained. "This is their Jerusalem."

Relatively few Portuguese have ever walked across the Cape of Sagres and braced themselves against the hot violence of the sand-laden simoom wind, or stared in wonder across the small bay, fortified by implacable palisades, at the lighthouse atop the adjoining finger of land, Cape St. Vincent. Yet every Portuguese child knows Sagres and of how a young royal prince, Henry the Navigator, made this obscure corner his monastery-like home and the headquarters for pioneering explorations of the world. Prince Henry the Navigator was half Portuguese and half English, being the third of the five sons of King John I and Philippa, the daughter of John of Gaunt. While in his early twenties he organized the expedition which seized the Moroccan city of Ceuta from the Arabs in 1415, and then devoted the rest of his life to making his country the world's first great maritime power. He did not take part in explorations himself but provided the research, instruments, and the navigational training that made the Portuguese discoveries possible.

At Sagres, the young prince gathered together map makers and mathematicians, developed instruments for taking bearings on the heavens, and welcomed sailing men who could tell him about their experiences on the water. From Sagres he sent ships across the oceans, opening the

A statue in Lagos of Prince Henry the Navigator, who promoted and guided Portugal's early maritime explorations

great century known as the Age of Discovery, which carried his country's flag to unknown lands from Madeira to India, brought excitingly new exotic products to his people, and bequeathed a nagging feeling of melancholy to modern-day Portuguese, causing them to wonder whether ever again they will be in the vanguard of civilization's forward movement.

Five Hundred Years Later

Today, more than five centuries after Prince Henry's death, the Cape of Sagres has a melancholy look. The railroad does not go any closer to it than Lagos, the old Moorish fortress town, 20 miles away. Several times a day a bus travels from Lagos to the center of the fishing village that calls itself Sagres, skirting the lonely cape where Henry the Navigator used to stand and look out to sea. The Cape of Sagres is so flat and solid that it looks like the result of a massive landfill operation. A long road, of the type that connects an Arizona desert highway with a distant ranch-house, leads to the end of the cape which is hidden by a high-walled fortress surrounding the historic complex where Henry the Navigator lived, worked, and saw many of his dreams come true. Inside the stockade-like enclosure are the remains of the royal prince's settle-

The famous Rosa dos Ventos, the rudimentary compass of stones constructed by Prince Henry the Navigator at Sagres to instruct the explorers he was sending to sea

ment of pioneers: the single-story structure with the trim row of slotted Moorish chimneys that was the navigational school and is now a youth hostel, a white-façaded chapel with belltower that could have been built for a movie set but was not, and a protective battlement offering wide-angled views that end only when the sea and sky meet. Spread out on the dusty ground, like the parachute of an astronaut just returned from outer space, is a reconstruction of the Rosa dos Ventos, the immense compass of stones that Henry used in instructing the men he was sending to sea. Portugal was born and baptized in the north but in the south, at Sagres, its life was given purpose.

The only seagoing activity at Sagres today centers around the fishermen from the village, two miles east of the cape. The village, a collection of whitewashed houses, a new refrigeration plant with a large representation of St. Joseph painted on the outer wall, a modern hotel, and a few miscellaneous shops, gets as close as possible to the edge of the cliffs which circle the small cove used by the fishermen. Each morning fishermen and nonfishermen cluster in small groups on the beach— the women separated from the men. Several national policemen, dressed as smartly as if they were on duty in Rossio Square in Lisbon, stand patiently in the sun, talking about Benefica, or some other football team, and its chances for bringing Portugal the World Cup some day. Nuzzled in the sand of the beach are old wooden boats with paint peeling. The people on the beach are almost as motionless as the boats. Suddenly, the fishermen decide it is time. Singing and shouting, some wearing boots and others in bare feet with pants rolled above their knees, a dozen of the fishermen push one of the open wooden boats into the water and gingerly climb into it. They set off as if going on an excursion, waving and calling to the people on the beach. Several other boatloads of fishermen join them in retrieving the nets that had been set out the night before a short distance from the shore.

Within a half hour, they begin their return, but now there is no hubbub or happy tumult. Everyone is serious. In twos the fishermen wade to the shore, carrying huge nets shaking with the futile movements of fish, and empty them on the sand before the onlookers who watch expectantly. There are hake, squid—all kinds of fish—and each rates its own spot on the sand, separated from a neighboring mound by several feet. When, after a quarter of an hour, all the fishermen have dumped their catch on the ground, the policemen and the onlookers crowd around the first pile of fish in a football-huddle formation. Some of the fish are still flapping their fins and those near the bottom of the pile are caked with sand, as if ready for the oven. Everyone stares at the helpless fish and an old man calls off figures swiftly. Then, getting a signal from someone in the crowd, he moves to the next pile of fish to be auctioned off while the policemen write down the price that the previous batch went for. The presence of the policemen assures order, and the day's fish auction is over in less than 30 minutes. Housewives scoop up at bargain prices the fish passed over by the restaurant men and professional buyers.

The Algarve

Sagres is in the Algarve, the most southern of the five provinces in the lower half of Portugal. As one moves from the north to south the rain becomes scarcer, the sun brightens, and the sky turns bluer. There are several groupings of mountains, such as those near Lisbon and in the western Algarve, but south of the Tagus is generally a wide-open area that is cultivated by paid workers who live their lives on huge estates or are hired from neighboring villages. Some estates have thirty or forty thousand acres; others, four or five hundred. This was the last area reconquered from the Moors and many Moorish customs and traits have lingered among the people.

It is a particularly traditional area, especially in regard to the role of women. Women can toil in the fields, carry things on their head, and wash clothes on the banks of the nearest body of water but this does not mean that they are ever left to fend for themselves. Tradition protects them. Young girls do not go to a village dance without having a married woman along with them. In some parts of the south a housewife who has girl servants must promise their mothers that she will see to it that all doors to the house are securely locked at night. A woman cannot get a passport to travel abroad unless she has the permission of her husband in writing. All these customs, however, do not make the

178

(Above) The morning's catch is hustled ashore by these fishermen at Sagres in southern Portugal

(Below) At the fish auction, a national policeman keeps order while the auctioneer (in beret) conducts the proceedings

women coolly indifferent or unresponsive. They smile, laugh, return a stranger's greeting with a pleasant *Bom Dia,* and if a tourist happens to take their picture on a street corner or a village road with great sincerity they will say *Muito Obrigado.* Every person in Portugal—there might not even be one exception—is friendly, hospitable, cordial, and helpful to strangers. The friendliness and warmth sometimes come as a surprise because at first glance the average Portuguese looks somber, if not severe. Even in the sunny south, where one might expect the personalities of the people to match the open sky and warm land, faces are often blank masks. But once communication is established the Portuguese speedily radiates a friendly warmth that is obviously real.

As one goes from north to south the vegetation changes, too, and here at the southern end of Portugal, figs, sugar cane, lilies, dates, almonds, agaves, and other tropical fruits and plants flourish in the balmy climate. North Africa is next door, while north Portugal—even Lisbon—seems far away. Farm women dress in long black cloaks, often

The beachfront at Estoril, the haven of former crowned heads and now both a popular resort area and a favorite spot for fishermen outside Lisbon

Salt-reclaiming beds along the waterfront in the Algarve, near Faro

with their heads hooded like Orthodox nuns in the Middle East, and stand in the shady side of a doorway or behind a screen-like, wooden Persian blind, satisfying their female curiosity to see what is taking place around them but at the same time remaining virtually invisible to the eyes of others. The houses and farm buildings are white, but often trimmed with another color in broad bands. Mules traveling in a circle 20 feet in diameter provide the power for drawing from wells water that is scooped up by the bucketful and funneled to fields of vegetables. Dreary railroad stations are brightened by flower gardens and by birds in cages hanging near the entrance. Close to the Spanish border, in the flatlands along the seaside, are big rectangular beds for reclaiming salt from the ocean. In recent years the Portuguese government has been encouraging the development of the Algarve as a tourism center, and many hotels, some quite luxurious, have been built.

Agricultural Provinces

The Tagus has given its name to three of the southern provinces and Baixo Alentejo, meaning "the low one below the Tagus," is the largest province in Portugal. Most of the land is in the hands of a few and it is

181

farmed in a manner reminiscent of feudal times. The estate of the land-owner, the *monte,* is often the complete world for many of the farm workers, just as in some cases it was for their parents and grand-parents before them. Houses, dormitories, workshops, barns, stables, dining halls—all are grouped together around the home of the land-owners. The pay is not high, but the workers are guaranteed a place to eat and sleep, and soon they acquire a proprietor's interest in the fate of the farm. In the evening when they are eating or afterwards when they are staring into a blazing fireside, they refer to "our cows," "our fields," "our next crop of cork," as if the farm was a profit-sharing enterprise. But this comfortable feeling that everyone—owner, crafts-man, cook, seasonal worker—is part of the one household does not undermine the class structure which is a foundation of Portuguese life. There is always the basic and wide distinction in Portugal between the boss or the master and the person working for him.

This province also houses Alcácer do Sal, the site of the last major stronghold of the Moors. The Moorish garrison left their mark on Portugal in a unique way. A Portuguese nobleman, in the attack on Alcácer do Sal, captured the pretty daughter of the Moorish governor and, falling in love with her, asked his king for permission for them to get married. The king agreed provided that the young woman became a Christian—which was the standard practice in the era of the Recon-quest—and he gave the couple land near Leiria, north of the Tagus, as their domain. The nobleman named the fief granted to him after his Moorish wife, Fatima, and the name remained with the village which grew up there.

Like its larger sister to the south, Alto Alentejo is practically free of mountains and is one vast plain on which cork trees supply much of the scenery. With the skill of a surgeon, farm workers cut the bark from the trees in long, wide strips, doing their part to preserve Portu-gal's reputation as the world's greatest exporter of cork. The men wear big, high-crowned hats as a protection against the sun, and the women often screen their necks by tucking a large handkerchief under their hat and letting it drop, like a curtain, on their shoulders. Like Bedouins of the Middle East deserts who know the strange workings of the sun, the men and women in the fields of the Alentejo are inclined to wear as much clothing in the summer as in the winter.

Another remarkable difference between the north and the south halves of Portugal is in the practice of religion. In the north the people have their small farms, live a quiet rural life in the traditional way, and most of them go to church. In Lisbon church-going suffers the same fate as it does in other metropolises of the world today, and attendance at Sunday Mass is less than 20 per cent. South of the Tagus, attendance shrinks to 5 per cent or less, and very few men are among the church-goers. The lack of priests is one answer. South of the Tagus there is only one priest for every 7,000 people, whereas the European average is one for every 900. South of Évora, the main city of this province, some pastors are in charge of as many as a half dozen widely scattered parishes, and to be in charge of three or four is normal. The long complex church-state history in Portugal has been a factor. Some describe the people of the south as "de-Christianized" while others say they are as religious as anyone else, except that they do not go to church. The

Freight cars on a siding at Badajoz in western Spain are tightly packed with bales of cork. Although Portugal is the world's greatest exporter of cork, the entire Iberian peninsula is rich in the agricultural resource

Jesuits, who have been suppressed in Portugal several times, opened a School of Advanced Studies for businessmen at Évora in the mid '60s. It was an interesting milestone in their history because just a few years earlier, in 1959, they observed two significant centenaries: the 400th anniversary of the original founding of their University of Évora and the 200th anniversary of its suppression by the Marquis de Pombal.

Tomar, one of the oldest towns in the province of Ribatejo, on the banks of the Tagus, was W. Somerset Maugham's favorite place in Portugal. If this is not enough recommendation, attendance at its Tabuleiros festival, held every fourth summer, could be the convincer. This festival, full of symbolism and ancient meanings, goes back probably as far as the sixteenth century. Girls in pure white dresses carry on their heads, in a procession, a stack of several dozen loaves of bread, each weighing a pound or more, that are laced together by rods and embroidered with bright crimson flowers and sprigs of green. The important thing is that each stack must be as tall as the girl carrying it. In olden times the Tabuleiros were offered by pious people to the Holy

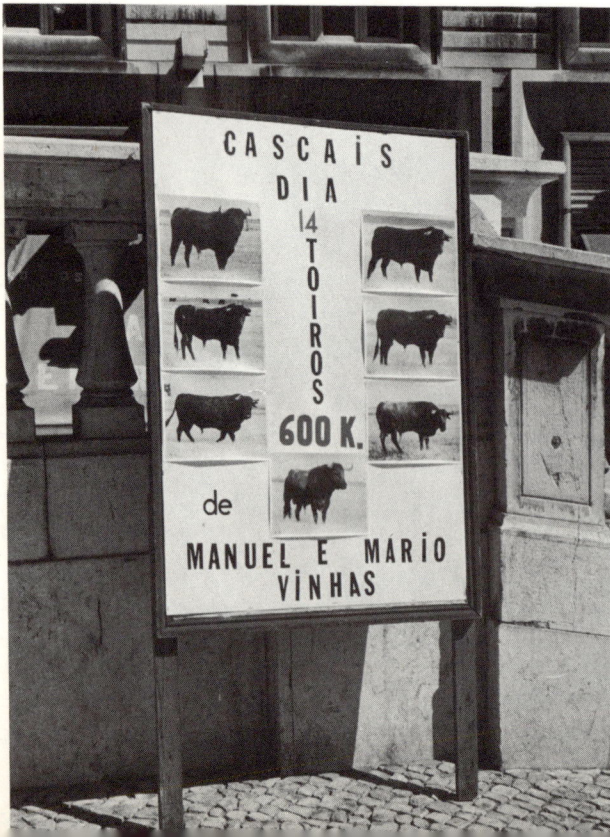

Advertisement for a bullfight at Cascais, a resort near Lisbon. The "600 K." refers to the bulls' weighing 600 kilograms, a particularly heavy weight

Spirit in return for, or in requesting favors. Although a dove, representing the Holy Spirit, is still carried atop each stack, the festival is nowadays more traditional than religious. It is a long weekend of bullfights, dances, and fireworks.

A famous dance of the province is the *verde gaio,* a combination square dance and reel that is danced in quick tempo and spirit, often to the tune of an accordion. The men have their dance, too, a lively fandango. A man does the fandango by himself and if he is a good dancer, and the spirit moves him, his quick toe spells out the word *amor* on the ground. The province has a long tradition for rugged sports and Vila Franca de Xira is Portugal's bullfighting center. Practically every village in the province has a bull ring, and more than enough bullfight enthusiasts to fill the viewing stands.

Lisbon

Part of the province of Estremadura is below the Tagus, part of it is above, and all of it is overshadowed by the city of Lisbon. Each town has its special *festa.* At Nazaré, which some say was once inhabited by the Phoenicians, fishermen each year festoon their boats with homemade decorations to remember the time when a hunter, about to tumble to his death because the edge of the cliff was crumbling under him, instinctively appealed to Nossa Senhora, and was saved. Portuguese have a unique way, and a long tradition, for making *ex voto* offerings of thanksgiving. At Mafra King John V, in return for an heir that he had prayed for, built a monastery dedicated to St. Anthony, and it is the largest memorial in the world honoring the Lisbon friar.

Titles for the Portuguese capital are many, and "Princess of the Tagus" seems the most fitting because, even though the river is at its widest here, the city of Lisbon easily dominates it. In 1966 the Tagus was harnessed by a 3,323-foot bridge connecting Lisbon with the Setúbal peninsula (on the left bank), and opening up a brand-new, shorter route to the area south of the Tagus. It is a record-sized bridge (longest bridge span in Europe, highest bridge towers, and so forth) but its chief impact is that it speeds traffic across the river. Previously the only way to get from one side to the other was by ferry or by going upstream to the bridge at Vila Franca, 15 miles away.

Another new addition to the Lisbon skyline is the tremendous Christ-the-King statue on the left bank, between the bridge and the ferry terminal. The base of the statue is 266 feet high, and the statue itself is 91 feet, so it is a most noticeable landmark. It was unveiled in 1959 following the promise of the Cardinal-Patriarch of Lisbon that he would build such a monument of thanksgiving if Portugal escaped occupation by the Nazis in World War II.

The view from the bridge is magnificent. Looking downstream, one marvels at the way the Tagus, after having widened into a huge bay, gives the appearance of waiting patiently in line to squeeze through a narrow channel in order to enter the Atlantic. The golden color of its sand-filled waters has given the river basin the name "sea of straw." Electric subway trains that cost 4 escudos in second class and 6 escudos in first class snake along the 15-mile waterfront between Lisbon and Estoril, the haven of former crowned heads and some hoping one day to be crowned, which is west of Lisbon just beyond the mouth of the Tagus. In the shadow of the bridge, a few hundred yards downstream in the Belém section of Lisbon, is a monument to the Discoverers, installed at the point where the caravels were built that took them on their explorations. Just inland from the waterfront monument is the long, spectacular Jerónimos monastery, erected as a thanksgiving offering for the discovery of the sea route to India, and now the burial place of Vasco da Gama. The monastery is lavishly embellished with finely formed stone representations of anchors, coils of rope, ship lines, tropical plants and flowers, and other objects associated with the discoveries in the distant lands. The monastery is a superb example of the exultant Manueline architectural style, named after the Discovery King, Manuel I, during whose reign the discoveries and explorations, set in motion by Prince Henry the Navigator a century earlier, reached their greatest success. But King Manuel, for all the good he did his

The towering Christ the King statue on the left bank of the Tagus at Lisbon was erected as a thanksgiving offering for Portugal's neutrality in World War II

186

country with the explorations abroad, hurt it at home by introducing the Inquisition and by ending the humanitarian refuge which Portugal had become for the Jews driven out of Spain by Ferdinand and Isabella. In order to marry the daughter of the Spanish monarchs he agreed to their demand that the Jews who had fled to Portugal should be forced either to become Christians or be expelled. The Jews left Portugal and were welcomed in such new havens as Amsterdam where, with skill and faith, they built what is known today as the Portuguese Synagogue, one of the world's most beautiful houses of God.

The Setúbal peninsula is fast developing as a center of industry, thanks to its accessibility because of the new bridge, and its biggest industrial resident is the ever-expanding national steel company. Looking upstream, toward Vila Franca, one sees that the right bank of the Tagus is like one long assembly plant of smokestacks, work yards, factories, cranes—the whole panoply of industry. General Motors and Ford are neighbors in this indusrial row that stretches 15 miles up the Tagus, assembling in big plants their European models imported from Germany and England, but using locally made parts, such as tires and electrical pieces, as much as possible. Seven European automobile companies have plants along here, happy for the availability, skill and relative low cost, of manual labor from the neighboring villages. In Portugal, the higher the labor content of a product the cheaper is its price.

Daily Life and Customs

Lisbon is a city of soft colors, of pinks, of blues, and of greens, whose shades change according to the whims of sea and sun. The 1755 earthquake shook up the city and many of its oldest buildings vanished forever. The Marquis de Pombal, who was the head of the government at the time, laid out broad new boulevards and directed the rebuilding of the city so that it emerged from the rubble, like a modern Phoenix, with new life, allure, and hope. The ship is the natural symbol of Lisbon and it is seen on lamp posts and on street signs.

At Cais do Sodré, where the electric subway train leaves for Estoril, is a huge public market. It is open daily, including Sundays until 2

188

o'clock, and is a main shopping area for housewives not only of downtown Lisbon but also of the suburbanites who have to take a ferry or train to get home. Chickens are sold dead or alive, with the price of a *vivo* somewhere around 24 escudos and a *morto* costing a half dozen escudos more. Live rabbits nestle on counter tops, calmly ignoring the shoppers who are sizing them up as a Sunday dinner possibility. Since it is a public market it stocks every type of food, and although one might have to wait in line and shop at a number of stands—oranges here, cheese there, olive oil in the far corner, and so forth—the prices are better than in neighborhood shops. The market also offers for sale what are probably the longest fish available to shoppers in the Western world—a fish that resembles a pike, and is more than a yard long. Piled in mounds are whole pineapples, a product of the Azores which were discovered by the Portuguese in 1440.

The people of Lisbon like to eat, and fish and poultry are their usual foods, both because they like them and because the prices are good. They like salads, too, and they perk up a plate of lettuce with thin crescent-shaped slices of onion. Potatoes are extremely popular and, like the Danes, Lisbonites think nothing of eating one or two kinds— fried and boiled, for instance—at the same meal. Restaurant owners have a subtle way of easing matters for the gourmand who wishes to appear as a normal eater. Items on the menu are followed by two price listings: one for a half portion, the other for the full portion. The latter is really a double portion but as long as no one admits to that no psychological harm is done. The cleanliness of the Portuguese is demonstrated in their restaurant habits. Just inside the doorway of many Lisbon restaurants is a lavabo, or a sink. As soon as a regular customer enters the restaurant he washes his hands with soap and water, almost ritualistically, and dries them in full view of the diners. No one seems to be troubled by using the same soap and towel as everyone else.

Lisbonites are serious coffee-drinkers. They have their favorite café which serves their favorite coffee—perhaps a blend from Angola, or maybe the strong product of Timor. They might drink it black from a small cup, or mixed in a small or large cup with milk. Or, they might

(Above) Flower vendors in
the Don Pedro IV Square in
the heart of Lisbon

(Below) Young Lisbonites
get a helping hand up a
steep hill by hanging onto the
upwardbound trolley

ask for it—either black or with milk—to be served in a glass. The women of Lisbon generally prefer tea, which has the Arabic-sounding name of *chá*, served in a silver pot with enough for two cups. Several small packets of sugar accompany each serving of coffee or tea, because Lisbonites have a sweet tooth.

The number of automobiles is gradually increasing, and all the car-making countries of western Europe are represented on the Lisbon streets. Taxi drivers prefer Mercedes, while the police crouch in Volks-Wagens. Most Lisbonites move from one part of the city to the other by bus, or trolley car. Fares are scheduled on a zone basis, but are low. The average trip is rarely more than an escudo. There is no array of advertising cards as in an American bus, but riders encounter such posted warnings as: "Whoever talks with the conductor (motor-man) makes himself morally responsible for the accidents caused by his being disturbed." Although the busses are double-deckers there is much queueing up because the number of standees is limited. No standees are allowed at all on the upper deck, and only four are permitted on the main floor. This is spelled out by a printed notice in the busses which says: "On 6 February 1956 His Excellency the Minister of Communications approved a regulation for permitting four standees on the main platform of two-level busses on condition they stand at the white posts provided as support." A map accompanying this announcement pinpoints the four locations where standing is authorized.

Formality and the Class System

This sounds quite formal but the Portuguese are a formal people. Even the language they speak is formal. It contains the familiar "you" form, *tu,* used in families and among close friends, but it does not have anything corresponding to the *Usted* that the Spanish use for general conversation with nonintimates. There is a *Voce,* that was brought from Brazil, but since it is used by the poor and the country people of the north it is avoided by educated Portuguese. Because of this linguistic situation they use the third person a great deal. If talking to someone named Pereira, for instance, a Lisbonite will say: "What does Mr. Pereira think about this?" If Mr. Pereira was unfamiliar with the Portuguese habit, his first reaction might be: "I don't know. Let's ask him." Even Portuguese on a first-name—but not a *tu*—basis will use this oblique method of address. Roberto Pereira, for example, would be asked: "What does Bob think about this?" Maids will refer to their employer as "Mr. Doctor," "Mr. Engineer" (*Engineer* is an important title in Portugal), or even "Your Excellency." There is a certain standoffishness in all relations. This formalism, a Lisbon resident observes, is comfortable and keeps everyone in his place on the social ladder.

Portuguese names can be long and at one time were *very* long. But since the '30s there has been a limit to the number of names a child can be given. Three is the average limit, and four is the most that will be accepted—two from the mother's side and two from the father's. Here is an example. José Manuel Monteiro Lisboa de Carvalho Marques is a Lisbon law student in his late twenties. The maiden name of his wife was Maria Manuela de Barros Casimiro de Almeida Dias. (Her grandfather, Manuel Casimiro de Almeida, was a famous bullfighter.) Since her marriage her name is Maria Manuela Casimiro de Almeida de Carvalho Marques. Their young son is named Miguel Casimiro de Almeida de Carvalho Marques.

About 100 families, it is said, run Portugal. Until recently the middle class has been very small and the majority of the people were workers and farmers. But, particularly in the Lisbon area, the ratio between the middle and the worker-farmer classes has been changing. Everyone is trying to climb higher on the social ladder or at least get a firmer foothold at his present level. Servants can no longer be taken for granted. They will quit a domestic job for a better-paying one in a factory, and they ask increasingly higher wages. Live-in cooks now seek 800 to 1,000 escudos a month—not a large sum, but it is nearly double what it was in the mid '60s. Inexperienced country girls working as maids are being paid between 400 and 500 escudos a month.

Luis Marques, a jolly newspaper editor who was born in Lisbon in 1898 and is married to Susan Lowndes, a grandniece of Hilaire Belloc, tells a story of how enthusiastically a Portuguese housewife talked to a visiting American professor about the labor-saving devices in the

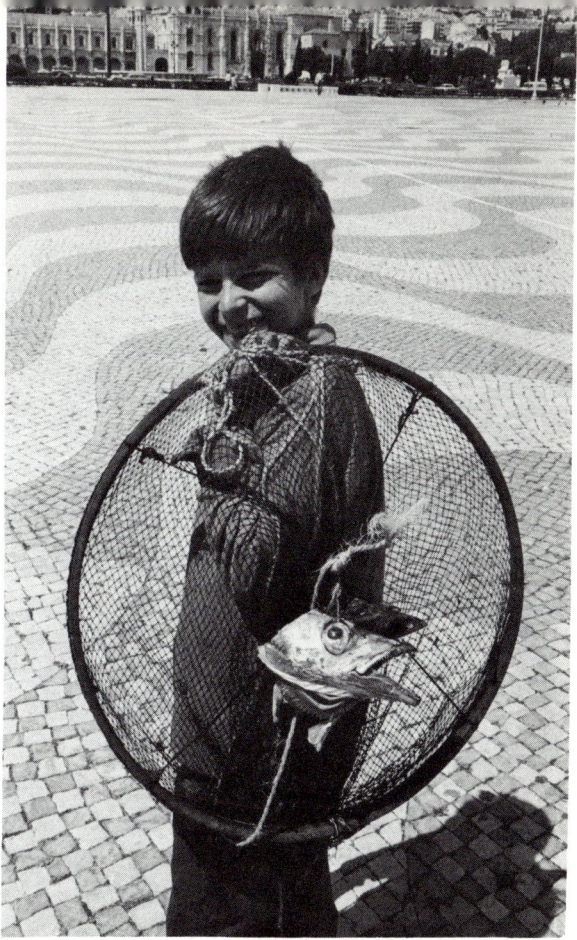

Although the rest of the fish was apparently eaten at home, a Lisbon boy retains its head to prove how big it was

United States. "Senhora," the professor remarked. "There is no better labor-saving device than a servant." However, the trend in Portugal is toward a servantless future, and the American-styled labor-saving devices.

Education and Religion

Education will speed the trend. Portuguese children start school when they are seven, and since 1964 have to attend school for at least six years. Previously, compulsory attendance was for only four years. School is free in the primary grades (the first six) but moderate fees are charged for upper grades. However, the government provides some Secondary School scholarships for promising students. After four years in the Escola Primária (Primary School), students planning a higher

193

education enter a *Liceu* (Secondary School), for a five-year course. Those intending to go to a university take a two-year pre-university (preparatory) course after finishing the regular *Liceu* program. *Liceu* students are required to study two foreign languages. Lisbon has a large institution for advanced technical studies, which is often referred to as a technical university, and throughout the country the number of vocational and commercial schools is being continuously increased. Since the Concordat with the Holy See in 1940, Religion has been in the curriculum of the state schools—the ones attended by most Portuguese children—but parents can ask for their children to be excused from the class. No arrangements are provided, however, for the religious instruction of Jewish or non-Catholic students.

Religious education will probably cut down on the devotion some pious people have for the *Santos de Cera*, the "Wax Saints." Possibly as a development of the traditional practice of monarchs of raising great monuments and monasteries as thanksgiving for their prayers being answered, a number of Lisbonites present objects of wax at the shrine or altar of a favorite saint along with their prayers. It might be an arm in wax, a leg, the breast of a woman, or the tiny form of a baby. The wax reproduction is meant to remind the saint of the physical favor they ask—what part of the body needs healing—or to thank him for having already replied to their prayers. The ceiling of a shrine in the Church of Nossa Senhora de Graça, not far from the Lisbon cathedral, is hung with dozens of such wax objects, and they can be found in other churches, too. Priests usually remove them and try to explain to the people that misguided devotion can become more superstitious than religious.

Sports

Football is extremely popular with Lisbonites, both as a spectator and as a betting sport. On Saturday nights a major bank in Don Pedro IV Square in Lisbon stays open till 2 a.m. so that Lisbon men might have enough time to consider how the next day's football games will turn out, and can fill in their three-escudo betting card accordingly. The early-morning atmosphere at the downtown bank is as solemn as

194

that in a Las Vegas gambling casino when big betting is taking place. Profits from the football lottery are used for such social-welfare purposes as hospital equipment, baby clinics, and so forth. It is about the only gambling allowed in Portugal. There are no horse races, and no dog tracks, and the gambling casino at Estoril is limited to foreigners.

During the summer there is a bullfight every Sunday, and Thursday evening is also bullfight time. As in Spain the bullfights are televised. The season opens at Easter in Lisbon and continues till St. Martin's Day (November 11) in Vila Franca. The Portuguese bullfighters dress in elegant costumes, designed two centuries ago, and wear a black tie in memory of a young nobleman who was killed in the bull ring in the eighteenth century and whose death brought a revision of the rules, making bullfighting safer though no less eloquent and prohibiting the death of the bull. One of the basic rules is fair play both for man and the beast. The bullfighter cannot strike the animal unless it is looking him in the eye.

Portugal's modern poet, Fernando António de Nogueira Pessoa, who happened to be born in Lisbon in 1888 on the feast of St. Anthony, loved his native city. In one of his poems he told about a man who walked through Lisbon as one strolls in the country, looking at houses, streets, and city sights the way one gazes at trees, roads, and flowers growing in fields in the countryside.

Anyone who does that in Lisbon will learn what the Portuguese mean by the word *saudade*, because even when he is far from this city in time and space, he will feel a strange yearning and nostalgia for the Princess of the Tagus.

The Future

Andres Peñalosa, a husky, 19-year-old pre-university student in the Basque city of San Sebastián, has liked motors all his life, and wants to be an automotive engineer. Spain does not have an advanced school for this, but Andres has heard of a good one in Milan and he has his heart set on going there. The automobile industry is growing fast in Spain, but Andres points out that all the cars coming off the Spanish assembly lines are made under foreign patents or licensing agreements. His idea is to get the best possible technical education abroad, return home, and work on developing his own car. Maybe one day, Andres speculates, he will be able to get a patent on a 100 per cent Spanish automobile.

He might indeed. If he does not the chances are some other young Spaniard will.

Spain's young people are dreaming and planning in positive, imaginative ways, and are reacting brightly to the world around them. They want to be an active part of it. The Civil War and its depressive divisiveness is something they never knew. To them it is an historical fact, at the most, and not a bitter, personal memory as it was for their parents when they were young. The new generation has grown up in the decade of the Spanish Economic Miracle, the dazzling era of international tourism when foreigners by the millions flood into the country, bringing a helpful supply of foreign currencies, of new ideas, and of friendly encouragement. Young Spaniards do not see any reason why the future cannot be even better, and they are planning and studying to make it so. It is the same everywhere on the Iberian peninsula.

Language laboratory at the Advanced Institute for Secretarial and Administrative Studies, in San Sebastián

The Woman's Role

The old concept of woman's place being exclusively in the home—a concept particularly strong in Spain possibly because of its Moorish heritage—is changing, and will keep on changing. Education is being made available not only to boys but to girls, and the old-time educational gap between husband and wife is narrowing.

A lovely young example of this trend is journalist Maria-Francisca Fernandez Valles, who was born in a Basque village in Guipúzcoa province and works on the San Sebastián daily, *La Voz de España*. Maria-Francisca graduated from the University of Navarre School of Journalism after a three-year course (it is now four years). She was 22 by the time she finished her studies in 1965, but a desk and typewriter in a city room were still months away. She could not go to work as a journalist until she passed an official examination. State examinations for all degrees are given in the university in which the student is enrolled, except in the case of journalism. To obtain the official title of "Journalist"—and without the title one cannot get a job as a journalist—candidates must take a three-day examination (written, practical, and oral) given by a tribunal of the Ministry of Information in Madrid, and before this have to complete a thesis. She chose as her thesis subject, "The Basque Statute in the Press of San Sebastián, 1931-1936." The thesis covered the period of autonomy given the Basque country by the Second Republic, and ended on July 18, 1936, the day that the Civil War began. Her idea was to demonstrate that the newspaper is the "fountain of history." She took four newspapers of different political tendencies to show the public how the various groups reacted to the same event. To be objective she read 7,000 individual newspaper issues.

Maria-Francisca is the first woman reporter on *La Voz de España*. It started as a summer job in 1966 and turned into a steady one.

"My mother was engaged at my age," Maria-Francisca says, "and like other young women of the time she could not go out without being accompanied by her fiancé. Today's generation goes everywhere—downtown, to Rome, or to Madrid. The young people of today know what they can do and what they cannot do, and they enjoy 'responsible freedom.' Their parents, too, know they are responsible young people."

Private Initiative

Another new attitude that augurs well for Spain's future is the way people are doing things for themselves, and not waiting for the government to do everything for them. Education is a fine example of this healthy new private initiative. The Spanish government gave education a high priority in its First Economic and Social Development Plan, and its goal is for every Spanish boy and girl to go at least as far as the university door. This ambitious plan, given a lift by the rising standard of living, has put great pressure on existing school facilities and has made it difficult for the government to keep up with the demand for education. In 1931-32, for example, there were 2,292,970 students enrolled from grade school through university. A quarter of a century later the over-all figure had more than doubled, reaching a total of 4,888,311, and the university enrollment of 121,289 was three times what it had been.

Rather than wait for the government program to catch up with the needs, private citizens in many cities of Spain have started schools on their own with official encouragement and aid. An example is at Oviedo, the capital of Asturias, where car-dealer Alfonso Acebal and 19 other fathers of families formed a nonprofit society in 1965, and obtained a 20-year loan at 2 per cent interest from the Ministry of Education to build a girls' school from kindergarten through pre-university. Three years later the building was finished, the first year of courses had been completed smoothly, and plans were mapped for making the school bigger. The original enrollment of a few dozen girls had grown to 300, and the new addition would increase capacity to 800. The number of fathers in the nonprofit society, meanwhile, had expanded ten times. The financing works out quite simply. Every father buys one share in the society for each of his daughters in the school. A share costs 25,000 pesetas, and does not change in value. These shares form a revolving fund.

When one child has finished school the cost of the share is returned to her father, and the share is purchased by another parent. Just as in any other private school, parents pay monthly charges which come to 1,500 pesetas for each girl and cover tuition, lunch, and school bussing. In the case of Señor Acebal this comes to 3,000 pesetas because his daughters (Pilar, 12; and Isabel, 11) attend the school. (His third child, Luis, is barred on two grounds: he is a boy and is only two years old.) Madrid parents have built two schools like this—one for boys; the other for girls. There are also two in Vigo; and others are in Barcelona, La Coruña, Pamplona, Córdoba, Zaragoza, and Lérida.

In the area just below Mount Tibidabo in Barcelona the school problem has been met in another way by other private individuals. The Costa y Llobera school, considered to be one of the best in Barcelona, is operated as a nonprofit enterprise, and students pay according to their means. It was started in 1957 in a dim flat on the Rambla Cataluña with 20 students, moved seven times in its first eight years, and now has a student body of 400 boys and a teaching staff of 40. Pablo Lopez Castellote, the director, and his associate, Pedro Darder, feel strongly about the importance of education.

Dr. Lopez, who is married and has four children, believes that schools should be a service to society and cannot be a commercial operation. The Lopez family lives on the upper floor of a walk-up apartment building about two miles from the school on the less fashionable end of the Avenida del Generalissimo. There are not too many rooms in the apartment, but Señora Lopez has furnished it invitingly, and signs of children are everywhere. There is no disorder, but there is a kind of agreeable informal order. Homemade rag dolls are propped up in beds, eyeing everyone and everything; home-drawn sketches and painted figures are thumbtacked to a bulletin board; and ceramic souvenirs from trips and outings lie, like family jewels, atop the long bookcase.

Tuition at the school can be as low as 900 pesetas a month, and as high as six or eight times that. But although a scale of tuition payments has been drawn up, none of these indicated tuitions is obligatory, and no sum is even indicated for families with incomes of less than 100,000 pesetas or those with more than 750,000 pesetas a year. Families on the lower end of the scale are assured that they do not have to pay the sum indicated, and those with higher incomes are equally advised that they can pay more than the *quota indicativa*. The according-to-one's means table was worked out after consultation with social economists and with the parents of students. Dr. Lopez points out that the table would not be practicable in a slum area but it can work out in a residential zone where there is a good cross-section of families.

There is a sliding pay scale for teachers, too, depending on the class they teach and their family status. The teacher salaries on this scale range from 7,500 to 8,700 pesetas a month. This is not high but it is higher than average—teacher salaries in Spain, as everywhere, are not high. Spanish teachers are paid by the hour. The teacher who teaches one hour a day will receive from 1,500 to 2,500 pesetas a month; a teacher with a two-hour daily schedule receives twice as much; and so on. Some teachers who are specialists will teach an hour in one school; the second hour in another; and so on. The legal ceiling is six hours a day, but there are teachers, it is said, who teach as many as 10 hours in order to build up their incomes. The extra-legal hours have to be limited to courses where state examinations are not required—such as "Recreation"—to prevent the detection of the "moonlighting."

Young boys at Tajamar, a vocational training school for boys in a shanty-town area of Madrid, are encouraged to develop trade skills early

At the Costa y Llobera school, all teachers have at least a three-hour daily schedule.

Artisans and Poets

The Spain of tomorrow is also going to have a generation of craftsmen who, now in their teens, are being encouraged and trained to use the kind of skills that have beautified and enriched their nation over the centuries. At Monte Alegre school, an Opus Dei institution in Asturias, for instance, 60 girl students take a three-year course in design that sweeps across a wide-ranging field—from windowdressing to TV and theater sets; from cigarette packages to garden furniture; from vases and bottles to covers for records. Similar schools are in Madrid, Seville, Barcelona, Bilbao, and Zaragoza. The tuition at Monte Alegre is 1,000 pesetas a month, and to enter it the girls must have finished their secondary education.

In a back street of a shabby *barrio* in Valencia, Vicente March Bernial, who has been awarded the national titles of *Artesano Ejemplar* and *Artesano Ilustre* for his design work, has a classroom for young boys of the neighborhood alongside the atelier where he and his family produce various works of religious and secular art. About 30 boys, aged from 10 to 18, crowd into the classroom every evening between 7 and 9 o'clock and at benches, under the guidance of Señor March or one of his six children, fashion articles from wood, metal, terra cotta, and any other material that suits their fancy. Señor March, the son of a sculptor, started the classes for the neighborhood youngsters 30 years ago. He is now 60, and his own children range in age from 15 to 26. The project has nothing to do with the government or the Church, or any organization. It is completely a voluntary private undertaking which gets moral and other support from well-wishers.

A new bookstore in Lisbon, the Galleria Quadrante, has introduced something new in communication between people—an idea not necessarily new elsewhere in the world but one which is brand-new in Portugal. One evening a week Portuguese poets are invited to the Galleria Quadrante to read their poems. This is not an autograph session, and there is nothing to buy. What is interesting is that after a poem has been read people in the audience ask questions. The poetry readings were started not long after the bookshop was opened in 1967 by a young couple who like books, Maria Alice Ferreira and her husband, Eduardo. They are planning to ask novelists and other writers to come to the Galleria Quadrante and read excerpts from their books. They hope that other bookstores will organize similar programs for the public. "It was necessary to begin, so we began," Maria Alice Ferreira says. "If we have followers, that will be fine."

The Good Life

Portuguese traditionally viewed education as the fruit of wealth—something that was made possible by riches—rather than a contributing factor to a higher level of life. But this concept is changing. Illiteracy, which ranged as high as 70 per cent or more in the '20s, has been reduced to about 15 per cent.

The generally lower standard of living in Spain and Portugal has been one of the factors which have kept them from being seriously considered for membership in the Common Market. Another factor is that Common Market members fear competition and the upsetting of current trade patterns. Spain, for instance, produces many of the agricultural products which Common Market member Italy has in abundance. In the meanwhile, Spain and Portugal belong to the Outer Trading Group of nations organized by Great Britain, and tourism revenue bulwarks their economies.

It is impossible to exaggerate the importance of tourism. This is especially so in the case of Spain's economy which the invasion of tourists in recent years has raised from a low level—and keeps on raising. As long as the tourists keep coming to "sunny" Spain, the future will remain "bright" for Spaniards. Perhaps the only thing that could divert tourists from the Iberian peninsula and send them off in another direction would be a political crisis in either of the two countries. While Portugal remains politically calm, labor demonstrations, student protests, and separatist activities have been on the increase in Spain—though not extensive enough so far to ruffle the waves of tourists.

203

Dr. Antonio Oliveira Salazar, who was replaced as prime minister in 1968 by Marcello Caetano

Salazar and Portuguese Politics

In the spring of 1968 Salazar marked two important anniversaries in his life on the same weekend. On Saturday he completed 40 years in office, and on the following day he celebrated his seventy-ninth birthday. There was no public observance of these anniversaries in keeping with Salazar's inveterate desire to stay out of the limelight. The following September, Salazar suddenly moved into that limelight that he had so long, and successfully, avoided. Salazar had undergone an emergency operation, it was announced, because of a head injury resulting from a fall. While the Portuguese were being reassured by medical bulletins about his condition, they were making their own prognosis on their nation's political health.

Then, on September 16, after it seemed that Salazar had reached the out-of-danger list, it was announced that he had suffered a para-lyzing stroke and had slipped into a coma.

For years the Portuguese had been asking themselves what would happen when Salazar was no longer prime minister. The position is appointive, and Salazar had never proposed a successor. The Constitution of Portugal says that the president appoints the prime minister. That is all. The severity of Salazar's illness raised the question of his successor from the realm of casual speculation to vital actuality. The president of the republic embarked on a series of consultations with prominent Portuguese, in and out of the government. The military authorities were consulted automatically.

Finally, eleven days after the grave illness of Salazar had struck, a close friend and a former minister in his government—62-year-old Marcello Caetano, a law professor—was appointed to take over the government as Portugal's new prime minister.

In his inauguration speech, made shortly after he and his cabinet were sworn in, Mr. Caetano managed to reassure conservative followers of Salazar that there would be no spectacular changes in the status quo and at the same time gave liberals a hope that some changes would be made.

Signs of possible change were not long in coming. A democratic opposition leader who had been exiled under Salazar was allowed to come home. The press was operating with greater freedom. New labor laws, permitting union members to select their representatives without official intervention, were expected. It was even thought that a place would be found in the tight government setup for the long voiceless democratic opposition.

Even the slightest change or movement toward greater freedom under the new government will be hailed at home and abroad as a significant milestone. Future historians will probably say that Salazar formed the country in his own image so that it reflected his likes and dislikes instinctively. Even Portuguese in their fifties cannot remember any other government except the Salazar one. He was called the "quiet dictator," but his presence was felt. If there had to be criticism, Salazar wanted it offered quietly and privately. He did not approve of the press being a force for public linen-washing. As a result the newspapers of Portugal did not attack nor criticize during Salazar's long reign; they concerned themselves with nonpolitical matters, such as girls, football, and the cinema. The newspapers were wary, too, of carrying foreign news that might displease. In the summer of 1968, for instance, a major Lisbon newspaper ran a banner headline reporting that French Prime Minister Pompidou would probably be replaced. In parentheses in the same big headline, it added: "Government sources say." This is not the usual way to write a headline but it is a politically safe way.

"Politics has been abandoned in Portugal," is a term used to describe the Portuguese political system. Political parties do not exist. There is a *Uniaõ Nacional* ("National Union") which is generally dormant except at election time when it submits lists of candidates for the National Assembly. Sometimes there are local lists, too, but this is a difficult process. The government drafts and selects the bills that go to the National Assembly for consideration and enactment. Before a bill is sent to the National Assembly it is first debated privately in the Corporative Chamber, a nonelective group of representatives of local autonomous bodies and social interests, such as banks and trade unions.

The Political Constitution of the Portuguese Republic, approved by national plebiscite in 1933 and modified by subsequent laws, specifies (Chapter II, Article 8) twenty "rights, liberties, and individual guarantees" which the citizens of Portugal shall enjoy. These include the "free expression of thought in any form," "freedom of teaching," and "freedom of meeting and association." But after these rights are enumerated, a following section states: "Special laws shall govern the exercise of the freedom of expression of opinion, education, meeting, and of association."

Limitations on freedom of speech are also provided for in Chapter VI, Article 22, of the Political Constitution which says: "Public opinion is a fundamental part of the policy and administration of the country; it shall be the duty of the state to protect it against all those influences which distort it from the truth, justice, good administration, and the common weal."

In regard to the press, the same chapter on "public opinion" says in Article 23: "The press exercises functions public in nature, and by virtue of this cannot refuse to print official news sent to it by the government on matters of national interest. A special law shall define the rights and duties both of newspaper companies and of professional journalists so as to safeguard the independence and dignity of both."

There are labor organizations but they have none of the freedom of movement and independence that is the right of American trade unionism. In regard to strikes or work stoppages, Chapter VIII, Article 39 of the Political Constitution says: "In their economic relations with each other, neither capital nor labor shall be allowed to suspend operations with the object of imposing their respective claims."

In general there was complete religious liberty under the Salazar regime, and the constitution itself assures freedom of worship and organization for all religious faiths. There is a *but,* however. The liberty does not apply to creeds "incompatible with the life and physical integrity of the human person and with good behaviour; or to the dissemination of doctrines contrary to the established social order." (Chapter X, Article 46.) The constitution does not identify which creeds could be "objectionable" and leaves it to the government to decide on an *ad hoc* basis.

Franco and Reform in Spain

Salazar never thought, of course, that he would be able to hold back the clock of political reform, but he tried slowing it down and succeeded. In Spain, Franco has not been as allergic to the winds of

General Francisco Franco, whose rise to power during the Civil War determined the course of Spanish politics for three decades thereafter

change. There has been some ground gained by Spaniards in the field of human and personal rights although this political progress has not moved at the same fast pace as the nation's economic advancement. In fact, political reform in Spain is often likened to a Spanish dance— three steps forward, two backward.

Franco and his associates are well aware of the criticism but they insist that they are the best judges of how fast and how far reform can go. "We won the Civil War in 1939," one of them will say, "without money, without nothing. Do you think we want to lose it now, 30 years later, when our country is getting back on her feet?"

The political arm that supported Franco in the Civil War was the Falange, founded in 1934 by José Antonio Primo de Rivera, the son of General Miguel Primo de Rivera, a dictator in the '20s. The Falange served as a foundation for the National Movement, a broadly based organization which in effect is a political party—and the only one. The role of the militant Falange in the National Movement has been shrinking ever since Spain started on its postwar recovery road. The leader of the National Movement is the head of state and its secretary general has the rank of minister in the government.

On the progress side of the ledger Spain has enacted a religious liberty law and has loosened the government's previous hold on the press and radio-TV communications. But such basic human rights as the formation of free trade unions by the workers and of associations by university students are still not permitted. As regards to free speech, Article 12 of the Fuero de los Españoles, says: "Every Spaniard may express his ideas freely provided they do not attack the fundamental principles of the state."

Vatican Council II, with the affirmative views it expressed on freedom of religion and of conscience, encouraged Spain to enact the religious liberty law which was adopted by the Spanish Cortes ("national legislature") in the summer of 1967 by an overwhelming vote. Previously the practice of non-Catholic religions was tolerated by the state but the law made it a positive legal right. The law affects the estimated 6,000 Jews, the 35,000 Protestants, and the small Moslem community in Spain. Non-Catholic ministers have not been altogether

208

satisfied with the law, fearing that the way it is worded might deny them the possibility of proselytizing.

In recent years the press has been given greater liberty. The Press and Printing Law of March 18, 1966, guarantees the press against prior censorship by the government and against obligatory consultation with government authorities except on major national security matters, such as in time of war. The dropping of press censorship, however, does not mean that the Spanish press is completely on its own. As in other countries of western Europe, steps can be taken against newspapers which print something that the government finds objectionable. In 1968, for instance, a Madrid daily newspaper was suspended twice, for a two-month period each time, for carrying articles that authorities objected to. This type of crackdown on the press is a losing proposition because the public is aware of what is going on—and does not like it. Even if a mechanical breakdown or a fire in a plant prevented delivery of a newspaper on the stands, the first reaction of the public would be that censorship blocked its appearance. On the Rambla in Barcelona one recent evening I asked for a copy of the American-owned *International Herald-Tribune*. It had not arrived from Paris, the newsdealer said, and when I asked why, he replied: *"Censura."* The casual bluntness of his answer prompted me to say: "Censorship? Really?" Looking me straight in the eye he said: *"Claro* (it's obvious)." A hundred-and-one factors could have prevented that day's edition of the American newspaper from getting from the plant off the Champs-Elyseés to the newsstand near the Gothic quarter in the capital of Catalonia. But as far as that newsdealer was concerned the reason was censorship.

The radio has been liberalized to the extent that regional stations can carry advertising and have greater program control. But in regard to news handling they have no autonomy whatsoever—everything emanates from Madrid. There are two major news broadcasts, one in the early afternoon and the other in the late evening. Spaniards, to amuse foreign friends at newsbroadcast time, will twirl the radio dial, sweeping across many frequencies. The same voice is heard on each station bringing the same news from the same news room in Madrid. All stations in Spain are plugged into one outlet at news time.

Nobody seems to mind this because the broadcasts are well done and highly professional, with two-way conversations between the commentator in the Madrid studio and correspondents in world capitals. The news is not censored but it seems to be selected in such a way as to give Spaniards the feeling that, when it is all said and done, things at home are no worse—and might even be better—than they are abroad.

Radio is considered a free enterprise in Spain and there are numerous local and regional broadcasting stations. But there is also an official radio service called Radio Naçional de España which has major stations in Madrid, Barcelona and Valencia, and outlets in most provinces.

In principle television is also a free enterprise but, in fact, the only existing TV service is operated by the state. There is no law, however, which says that the state is to enjoy a monopoly in this field. As with radio there are first-rate news and feature programs. Advertising is carried in both media—radio and TV. In fact, the average Spaniard says there are too many ads.

Dissent

Demonstrations by workers and by students are becoming progressively more numerous and less peaceful. Gunfire marked the Labor Day observance on May 1, 1967, and priests were among the many arrested in various parts of the country. There were mass demonstrations again on the European Labor Day the following year but this time the government assembled the largest number of security forces since Civil War days, and remained in control of the situation. Such demonstrations are organized by illegal workers' committees, *comisiones obreras,* to protest against wages and working conditions, and to force establishment of unions that are independent of the government-controlled "syndicates." The government says that Communist agitators are behind such demonstrations.

As in Rome, Paris, and other capitals, the university student population is in ferment in Spain. Students are seeking many reforms and one at the top of the list is freedom of association. There is only one approved student group, and this was organized by the government. Clashes between police and students in Barcelona and Madrid, in

210

particular, have been frequent in recent years, and have resulted in the closing of the universities in these cities at times. The student protest is not always directed against the government. After a big anti-Vietnam War rally on the Madrid campus in the spring of 1967, over 1,000 students shouting anti-American slogans and brandishing Vietcong flags, burned a half dozen American flags.

Spaniards, young and old, in all fields—priest, student, and worker —are increasingly making their voices heard, and will want a bigger voice in their government in the future.

This raises the critical question of what happens after Franco leaves the scene. The illness which brought Salazar's rule to an abrupt end magnifies the speculation about Franco's eventual successor. How will the succession in Spain compare to the way it has worked out in Portugal?

The Spanish Law of Succession

In Spain the situation is somewhat different but not any easier. Franco was born in 1892 and has headed the Spanish government since the end of the Civil War. On July 26, 1947, he provided the way for choosing his successor in the Law of Succession. In its first article the Law of Succession specifies that "Spain, as a political unit, is a Catholic, social and representative State which, in keeping with her tradition, declares herself constituted into a kingdom."

When the "headship of state" is vacant, the Law of Succession provides, the powers are assumed by a Regency Council which consists of the president of the Cortes, the highest-ranking prelate in Spain, and the heads of the army, navy, and air force. The Regency Council is to run the government until the new head of state—king or regent— is sworn in and takes office.

In accordance with the Law of Succession, Franco is authorized to name his successor. He can do this in any way he wishes, and at any time—in writing, in a will, and so forth. He does not have to pick a successor. If he does pick one, the choice might not necessarily become king. Franco can designate him as a Regent. No one knows what Franco has done, or will do.

The pretender to the throne is Don Juan de Borbon y Battenberg, now in his mid-fifties. Don Juan lives in Estoril but early in 1968 he visited Madrid for a week—his first visit in the Spanish capital in five years. The occasion for the visit was the christening of his first grandson but there was speculation that it really had something to do with the restoration of the monarchy. Another possibility as Franco's successor is Don Juan's oldest son, Don Juan Carlos. At the request of Don Juan many years ago, Don Juan Carlos has been educated by the Spanish government, and has attended all three service academies. Franco has increasingly taken Don Juan Carlos under his wing. In recent times Don Juan Carlos has been spending several weeks at each of the government ministries, has taken cruises on naval vessels, and has made inspection tours. All this is "for preparation," it is vaguely said. But preparation for what? No one says. At funeral ceremonies in the Escorial, and on other state occasions, Franco is escorted by Don Juan Carlos. But he also has with him Don Alfonso, the son of Don Juan's brother, Jaime.

Franco has kept everyone guessing, and no one knows what is in his mind. Perhaps he might step down and witness the swearing in of his successor, and Spain's new king. No one knows. In describing the character of people from different parts of Spain a Spanish observer says that if you meet a person on a stairway and do not know whether he is going up or down, you can be sure he is a Galician. Franco was born in Galicia.

The only thing sure about Franco's successor is that whether King or Regent he must be male and a Spaniard, at least 30 years old, and a Catholic. That is spelled out in the Law of Succession.

If there is a vacancy in the "headship of government," Spaniards are hopeful it will not last long because anti-monarchist and other elements might exploit the situation, and make a daring, bloody bid for power. The situation could get out of hand, and that would bring the army into the picture. But who would the army side with? Here again, all is speculation.

Other Books to Enjoy

GENERAL READING

All the Best in Spain and Portugal, by Sidney Aylmer Clark. New York: Dodd, Mead, 1966.

Complete Reference Guide to Spain and Portugal, by Pan American World Airways. New York: Simon & Schuster, 1967.

Geography of Spain and Portugal, by Ruth Way. New York: Barnes & Noble, 1962.

A History of Spain and Portugal, by William C. Atkinson. Baltimore: Penquin Books, 1960. (Paperback)

Iberians, by Antonio Arribas. New York: Praeger, 1964.

PORTUGAL

The Floating Revolution, by Warren Rogers. New York: McGraw-Hill, 1962.

Journals of a Residence in Portugal, 1800-1801, by Robert Southey. New York: Oxford University Press, 1960.

The Land and the People of Portugal, by Raymond A. Wohlrabe and Werner Krusch. Philadelphia: Lippincott, 1960.

A New History of Portugal, by Harold V. Livermore. New York: Cambridge University Press, 1966.

No Garlic in the Soup! by Leonard Wibberley. New York: Washburn, 1959.

Portugal, by Franz Villier. New York: Viking Press, 1963. (Paperback)

The Portugal I Love, by Michel Déon. New York: Tudor, 1963.

A Taste of Portugal, by Shirley Sarvis. New York: Scribner, 1967.

SPAIN

Adventures in Spain, by Alexandre Dumas. Garden City, N.Y.: Doubleday, 1959.

The Alhambra: Palace of Mystery and Splendor, by Washington Irving. New York: Macmillan, 1953.

Death in the Afternoon, by Ernest Hemingway. New York: Scribner, 1932.

Don Quixote, by Miguel de Cervantes. Baltimore: Penguin Books. (Paperback)

Explanation of Spain, by Elena de La Souchère. New York: Random House, 1964. (Paperback)

For Whom the Bell Tolls, by Ernest Hemingway. New York: Scribner, 1940. (Paperback)

Franco and the Spanish Civil War, by Laurence Ernest. New York: McGraw-Hill, 1968.

Iberia: Spanish Travels and Reflections, by James A. Michener. New York: Random House, 1968.

Spain, by Hugh Thomas and the Editors of Life. New York: Time, Inc., 1966.

Spain in the World, by Saxton E. Bradford. Princeton, N.J.: Van Nostrand, 1962. (Paperback)

Spain: The Root and the Flower, by John A. Crow. New York: Harper & Row, 1963.

Spain: The Vital Years, by Luis A. Bolin. Philadelphia: Lippincott, 1967.

Spanish Centuries, by Alan Lloyd. Garden City, N.Y.: Doubleday, 1968.

Spanish Civil War: Domestic Crisis or International Conspiracy?, by Gabriel Jackson. Boston: Heath, 1967. (Paperback)

Spanish Leaves, by Honor Tracy. New York: Random House, 1964.

Spanish Roundabout, by Maureen Daly. New York: Dodd, Mead, 1960.

The Sun Also Rises, by Ernest Hemingway. New York: Scribner. (Paperback)

Tales of the Alhambra, by Washington Irving. Indianapolis: Bobbs-Merrill, 1962.

Through Spain with Don Quixote, by Rupert Croft-Cooke. New York: Knopf, 1960.

Historical Highlights

Iberia

B.C.

ca. 10,000	First Iberian cave paintings in the Ebro valley
1100	Phoenicians found seaport of Cádiz
500-600	Celts occupy northwestern Spain, northern Portugal
218	Carthaginians occupy Spain. Romans enter to battle their rivals
146	Romans win Third Punic War and colonize Iberian peninsula
38	Romans completely control peninsula

A.D.

2	Philosopher Seneca is born in Córdoba
61-67	Christianization of Spain begun by St. James the Greater and St. Paul
414	Visigoths occupy Spain; Rome already in decline
589	During the Third Council of Toledo, Visigoth king Recaredo renounces Arianism, adopts orthodox Christianity
711	Moors invade Spain; Visigoth kingdom collapses
718	Reconquest of Spain from Moors begun in north by Asturian king Pelayo
912	Córdoba, seat of Moslem caliphate, becomes a main cultural center of Europe
1035	Death of Sancho the Great marks beginning of independent histories of Aragon and Castile. Intensification of Reconquest, growing religious fanaticism
1094	The Cid, El Conquistador, seizes Valencia from Moors, beginning a period of conquests for Castile and Aragon
1139	The establishment of the kingdom of Portugal, after death of Afonso VI of Castile, marks a period of anarchy and disunity due to the continued existence of individual states

Spain

1137 Spanish national unity encouraged by union of Aragon and Catalonia

1143 King of León recognizes kingdom of Portugal

1287 Afonso III affirms *Privileges of the Union,* officially recognizing a league of nobles. Increasing dissatisfaction with monarchy

1385 Portuguese defeat Spaniards at Battle of Batalha

1402 Canary Islands made part of Spain

1474 Accession of Isabella I ends anarchy in Castile. First Spanish book published in Valencia

1478 Holy Inquisition established to insure religious unity

1479 Castile and Aragon united when Prince Ferdinand of Aragon, husband of Queen Isabella of Castile, is crowned king of Aragon

1492 Columbus sails from Spain, discovers America. His sponsor, Isabella, be-

Portugal

1128 Afonso Henriques declares independence from king of León

1139 Afonso Henriques defeats Moors at Battle of Ourique and calls himself king of Portugal

1179 Pope Alexander III recognizes king of Portugal

1276 Portuguese Cardinal elected Pope John XXI

1373 Portugal signs alliance with England

1415 Overseas exploration and expansion begun with seizure of Ceuta in North Africa by Henry the Navigator

1418 Madeira and Azores archipelago discovered

1476 Portugal's opposition to accession of Isabella I to throne of Castile ends in defeat

1482 Exploration of Congo area

1488 Bartolomeo Diaz rounds Cape of Good Hope

214

Spain

comes founder of Spanish colonial empire. Conquest of Granada signals end of Moorish occupation. Jews ordered to become Christian or leave the country

1494 Spain and Portugal sign Treaty of Tordesillas. Portugal given wider area of discoveries than proposed by Pope

1515 Navarre united with kingdom of Aragon

1519 Charles I of Spain elected Holy Roman Emperor, Charles V. Spain becomes world power as a result of territorial acquisitions

1522 Hernan Cortez conquers Mexico, calls it New Spain

1525 Holy Roman Emperor Charles V defeats Francis I of France at Battle of Pavia

1535-1580 Conquistadores conquer Peru and Chile. Cities of Lima, Buenos Aires, and St. Augustine founded

1565 Philippine Islands added to the Spanish empire

1571 Ottoman naval power checked at Battle of Lepanto

1580 Philip II acquires Portugal through inheritance

1588 The "Invincible Armada" is defeated by England

1605 Cervantes publishes first part of *Don Quixote*

1640 Portugal and Catalonia revolt against Spain

1648 Thirty Years' War ends, marking decline of Spanish power. Independence of Holland recognized

1668 With England as intermediary, Portugal and Spain sign peace treaty; all conquered lands except Ceuta are returned to Portugal

1700 End of Hapsburg rule in Spain, followed by War of Spanish Succession

1701-1714 Final accession of Bourbon dynasty with Philip V

1713 Spain loses her European possessions, Flanders, Milan, Sicily, Sardinia

1808 Napoleon forces Charles IV of Spain to abdicate, awards throne to brother Joseph

1810-1824 Former West Indies gain independence; Spain's overseas possessions

Portugal

1492 Greenland discovered by Joao Fernandes, and Pedro de Barcelos

1497 King Manuel I orders Jews to become Christian or be expelled

1498 Vasco da Gama reaches India

ca. 1500 Golden Age of Portuguese Exploration marked with discovery of Brazil and Newfoundland

1522 Expedition led first by Portuguese Magellan and then by Basque Elcano sails around the world

1536 Establishment of "Tribunal of the Portuguese Inquisition"

1572 The *Lusíadas,* epic poem of Luiz de Camões, is published

1578 Catastrophe of Alcazarquivir. Dom Sebastian attempts to conquer Morocco; he and flower of nation perish

1580 Cardinal Henry, successor of King Sebastian, dies without naming successor. Spanish troops under Duke of Alba put down opposition, and Philip II of Spain adds Portugal to his realm. Spanish rule lasts 60 years

1640 Revolution ends Spanish rule; Duke of Braganza becomes King John IV

1662 Marriage of Catherine of Braganza to Charles II of England. Cornerstone of Portuguese foreign policy laid for centuries to come

1703 Methuen Treaty, commercial-political alliance with England. Portugal becomes a political protectorate of England during the 18th century

1755 Earthquake destroys half of Lisbon

1807 During era of French Revolution and Napoleon, Portugal incurs disaster as ally of England; therefore, regent Prince John transfers capital of Portugal to Rio de Janeiro

1821 King John VI returns to Lisbon; Prince Pedro remains in Brazil

1822 Prince Pedro calls for independence of Brazil, proclaims himself emperor

1825 John VI recognizes Brazil's independence

1826 Accession of John VI's granddaughter, Maria II, followed by struggles between constitutionalists and monarchists

1906 Dom Carlos accused of financial ir-

Spain

reduced to Cuba, Puerto Rico, and Philippines

1813   Spanish rebel against Napoleon, enlist British aid to drive him from peninsula

1873   First Republic created

1874   Monarchy restored

1879   Beginning of Socialist party and protest organizations. Prestige of the crown and the Church declining

1898   Spanish-American War; loss of Cuba, Puerto Rico, Philippines

1914-1918   Spain remains neutral during World War I; middle and upper classes enriched. After the war, depression sets in

1923   Military disaster in Spanish Morocco. Dictatorship established by General Primo de Rivera

1929   Rivera dismissed by Alfonso XIII, who loses support and leaves country in 1931

1931   The Second Republic; growth of extreme Right and Left factions

1936-1939   General Franco and others revolt against chaotic conditions in the country. Franco becomes dictator

1939   Franco aligns himself with Germany and Italy. Spain openly favors Axis during early years of World War II despite its neutrality

1946   Spain excluded from United Nations

1947   Franco becomes chief of state for life by Law of Succession, which re-establishes monarchy and provides for his successor

1950   Diplomatic relations with U.S., England, and France resumed

1951   Truman signs foreign aid bill allotting $100 million to Spain

1953   Spain signs a defense and economic cooperation agreement with U.S., a new Concordat with Holy See

1955   Spain admitted to U.N.

1956   Spain recognizes independence of Spanish Morocco

1964-1967   First Economic and Social Development Plan is successful

1968   African provinces of Fernando Poo and Rio Muni gain independence

Portugal

regularities; brief dictatorship under Premier Joao Franco

1908   Plans for reform cut short; dictatorship terminated by murder of king and crown prince

1910   Monarchy overthrown and republic established

1910-1930   Political rivalry; attempts to restore monarchy. Difficulties with Vatican due to anti-clerical nature of state

1911   Separation of Church and State

1913-1918   Relations with Rome broken off

1914-1918   During World War I, Portugal faithful to historic British alliance; takes active part on side of Allies

1916   Germany declares war on Portugal because of its aid to England

1926   Military coup d'etat. Salazar offered post of minister of finance, resigns in a few days because of limits on power

1928   Assured of free hand, Salazar joins Cabinet, four years later becomes prime minister

1933   Portugal's new constitution approved in plebiscite

1939-1945   Portugal tries to maintain neutrality during World War II; relations with Germany not broken until May, 1945

1940   Concordat with Holy See

1949   Portugal becomes member of NATO

1955   Portugal joins U.N.

1968   Salazar in his 40th year of government becomes seriously ill and is replaced as prime minister by a former associate, Marcello Caetano

Index

218

John V, King, 185

220

222

About the Author

DANIEL M. MADDEN, has been writing from Europe for United States publications, primarily *The New York Times, Catholic Digest,* and *Columbia,* for the past ten years. For six years before that he held a series of public information posts for the United States Government overseas, including those of Acting Director of Public Affairs in Austria and Director of Public Affairs in Belgium-Luxembourg.

Mr. Madden has written several books for young people; *Operation Escape* was selected by *The New York Times* as one of "100 Juvenile Books of the Year." An accomplished photographer as well as a writer, his photos have appeared on the covers of and inside many American magazines, and the pictures in this book were taken especially with the World Neighbor Series in mind.

World Neighbors

Written to introduce the reader to his contemporaries in other lands and to sketch the background needed for an understanding of the world today, these books are well-documented, revealing presentations. Based on first-hand knowledge of the country and illustrated with unusual photographs, the text is informal and inviting. Geographical, historical, and cultural data are woven unobtrusively into accounts of daily life. Maps, working index, chronology, and bibliography are useful additions.

ALASKA Pioneer State, by Norma Spring
ARGENTINA, PARAGUAY & URUGUAY, by Axel Hornos
AUSTRALIA & NEW ZEALAND, by Lyn Harrington
AUSTRIA & SWITZERLAND Alpine Countries, by Bernadine Bailey
BRAZIL Awakening Giant, by Kathleen Seegers
CANADA Young Giant of the North, by Adelaide Leitch
CENTRAL AMERICA Lands Seeking Unity, by Charles Paul May
CHILE Progress on Trial, by Charles Paul May
CHINA & THE CHINESE, by Lyn Harrington
EQUATORIAL AFRICA New World of Tomorrow, by Glenn Kittler
GREECE & THE GREEKS, by Lyn Harrington
INDIA Land of Rivers, by L. Winifred Bryce
ISRAEL New People in an Old Land, by Lily Edelman
ITALY Modern Renaissance, by Arnold Dobrin
JAPAN Crossroads of East and West, by Ruth Kirk
THE LOW COUNTRIES Gateways to Europe, by Roland Wolseley
MEDITERRANEAN AFRICA Four Muslim Nations, by Glenn Kittler
MEXICO Land of Hidden Treasure, by Ellis Credle
PERU, BOLIVIA, ECUADOR The Indian Andes, by Charles Paul May
SCANDINAVIA The Challenge of Welfare, by Harvey Edwards
THE SOVIET UNION A View from Within, by Franklin Folsom
SPAIN & PORTUGAL Iberian Portrait, by Daniel Madden
THE UNITED KINGDOM A New Britain, by Marian Moore
VIETNAM and Countries of the Mekong, by Larry Henderson
THE WEST INDIES Islands in the Sun, by Wilfred Cartey